KILLER BUDGIES

Mike Harding

Illustrations by Bill Tidy

ARROW BOOKS

Also in Arrow by Mike Harding

THE 14½lb BUDGIE
THE UNLUCKIEST MAN IN THE WORLD
THE ARMCHAIR ANARCHIST'S ALMANAC

Arrow Books Limited
17-21 Conway Street, London W1P 6JD

An imprint of the Hutchinson Publishing Group

London Melbourne Sydney Auckland
Johannesburg and agencies throughout
the world

First published by Robson Books 1983
Arrow edition 1984
Reprinted 1984 and 1985

© Mike Harding/Moonraker Productions 1983
Illustrations © Bill Tidy 1983

Printed and bound in Great Britain by
Anchor Brendon Limited, Tiptree, Essex

ISBN 0 09 937430 7

I had just finished my act at the Heckmondwyke Reform and Allotments Club, and walked off the stage to the comedians' anthem—the sound of my own footsteps—when an event occurred that was to transform my life and the lives of everybody in the world utterly and for ever.

My name is Chuckles, Eric Chuckles; stage name that is, my real name is Ron Burkitt. I worked the northern clubs as a comedian at nights, and during the day I worked as a quality controller in a factory that made sex-aids—I hit the blow-up rubber dolls to

3

see if eighteen-stone dockers could burst them, and tested the French ticklers out on shaved chickens. Everything I did in the clubs was so old that I paid tithes on it, and most of it appeared in first folio editions of the *Beano* and the *Dandy* in spidery italic. But I couldn't give a toss, as long as I made my twenty-five pounds a night following what looked like the same toothless, arthritic organist and the same geriatric drummer in clubs from Workington to Whitby, Stafford to South Shields.

'Eric Chuckles', my card said, 'a smile, a song and a balloon', while below was the address and telephone number of my agent and manager, Harry Gunk. Gunk had been on the boards himself—for twelve seconds. His act was so bad the audience had cited the Geneva Convention and beaten him senseless with wet crisp packets. Finding that he couldn't make a living out of himself, he turned to promoting others on their roads to ignominy and self-effacement. He became an agent, Barabbas, with a cigar. He was so bent he made Quasimodo look like a Burton's dummy, and had as much sense of honesty as a toad has feathers, but he was the only one who would handle Eric Chuckles. His office, at the top of a disused kosher bacon warehouse, looked like something that had come out of the last act of 'The Fall of the House of Usher'. The walls of his office were lined with fading photos of even more faded stars all signed 'To Harry—thanks for the good times—we did it our way'. Poor buggers! Pantomime in Wolverhampton, followed by variety in Sunderland, followed by a summer season in Redcar—you don't get that for murder nowadays.

Harry Gunk did all the bookings for this converted abattoir I was working at in Heckmondwyke, and he'd booked me in for a week. I opened the night with a twenty-five minute spot, interrupted only by the

4

knocking of dominoes on formica and the bronchial rattling of two hundred cloth-capped Bernard Levins and their attendant banshees. I died the death every night, and was followed by a gay Irish midget called 'Little Seamus Smiles from the Emerald Isle' who did Al Jolson numbers complete with the straw hat and cane. He sang 'Toot-toot-tootsie', 'Chattanooga-choo-choo', 'Ave Maria', 'Danny Boy' and a medley called 'Songs we sang in the shelters'.

The medley started off with a pre-recorded air-raid siren and finished off with 'Land of Hope and Glory' and the all-clear. Dear reader, I kid you not: he got so much applause that the rotten timbers of the club shook death watch beetles all over the punters —but no one bothered, they loved him. He was followed in his turn by a performing bird act. If there's anything I hate more than gay dwarfs it's bird acts and there we were, me and Seamus Smiles, the gay dwarf, and Rudolpho the Great and his Performing Budgies all cooped together in a dressing-room that had once been the coal cellar of the fire-lighter factory next door. I'd started off badly on the Monday night by taking the mickey out of one of the waitresses who was so ugly she made the beer go flat by looking at it. I came out with such comic gems as 'You could get a job frightening kids to bed...' 'I've never seen a face like that before, it's like a well used spade...' 'It should have road lamps round it...' None of these comedic jewels produced even the merest titter. It was only after I had died a very severe death that night that I learnt the reason why.

'Shun't 'ave picked on that lass son,' muttered the concert secretary. 'She got that face savin' a bus load of kids in a runaway bus from goin' in ter t'river. All our kids it were. She stopped it wi' 'er 'ed. Local 'ero she is.'

On Tuesday somebody in the front row slumped over and had to be carried out over the heads of the crowd. I thought he was drunk and took the mickey out of him for ten minutes. 'I'd like some of what he's had. Lean him against the wall—that's plastered too,' etc. Then the compere took the mike from my hand and said, 'We'll now have two minutes' silence for our treasurer Charlie Clegg who's just dropped dead in the front row.'

He handed me the mike back with a glare. I stood on stage for two minutes in dead silence then tried to carry on. It was like striking matches on wet tripe.

On Wednesday I told the filthiest jokes I knew thinking that was the way to get them. There were mass walk-outs amongst the audience. One lot of ladies demanding their money back were on a hen night from the local Catholic Church Legion of Mary. 'Youse can tell your man up dere wid de bucket mouth we'll be back to break his legs,' said their leader, a Mullingar lass with hands like hairy bananas. That night they smuggled me out in a beer crate.

By the time Thursday had come things had gone from bad to worse. Word had gone round Heckmond-wyke about how rubbishy I was, and people were turning up in droves to watch me sweat profusely and degenerate into gibberish every night. They'd given Seamus Smiles the first spot and moved me back to second spot to give them a chance to cram more people in to watch Eric Chuckles committing suicide with his mouth. Seamus Smiles didn't mind, it meant he could get home early leaving me to expire slowly from lack of talent before a gleefully malevolent public.

Crippin would have got more sympathy. That night I stormed into the dressing-room to find Seamus Smiles trowelling Pancake onto his face, and Rudolpho the Great slumped on the moth-eaten sofa with a bottle of cheap plonk in his hands. To say he drank is like saying that the Statue of Liberty's in New York. He drank so much that he was a fire hazard; if he'd gone teetotal there would have been mass suicides in the Highland malt whisky industry. I sat down in a tubular metal chair that was saying goodbye to its canvas seat, leaned back and lit a cigarette. 'What a karzi,' I muttered. 'I've seen better demolition sites.'

'Well, I don't know,' said Seamus. 'I've been in worse places dan this.'

'Where?' I asked, in amazement.

'Jayze, for the moment—thought escapes me—I'm having the mental blocks in me head. But I think Bognor Spa Pavilion takes some beating, or Morecambe Pier perhaps. I played Morecambe Pier de wanst with a terrible howling gale blowing—dere wuz so many holes in de pier de front row of the audience was two dozen seals.'

Rudolpho took a swig at the bottle. 'The trouble with you so-called comics and crooners,' he dribbled in a Home Counties, upper-crust, Hooray-Henry, hunt-the-fox, gin-and-tonic, Barbour-jacket, BMW-outside-the-pub-Sunday-lunchtime voice, 'is that you've never had it so bloody good. As far as the fish and chips brigade are concerned this is the London bally Palladium! We go on that stage every night and we give the silly old punters what they want and if we get paid it doesn't matter a hoot if they're rubbish or we're rubbish. My family motto is *pecuniaris et volent*—take the money and run. What more do you want than that? Art?' He turned away with a supercilious leer and started to run a nicotine-stained finger along the bars of the budgies' cages, making a maddening ringing noise until the poor birds leaped nervously from perch to perch, fluttering their wings piteously in fear.

I could have killed Rudolpho for the savage way he tormented those birds because, although I say I hate bird acts, I would never harm them. I hate the beady-eyed feathery little gets but I would never be cruel to them. But this swine Rudolpho was diabolical with them. He was all sweetness and light on the stage before the audience, getting the birds to pedal their little bikes and cars, pick out letters of the alphabet with their beaks and drive the little fire engines up and down and ring the little bells when they'd finished. Then he'd take a bow with them and kiss them all and pet them, but in the dressing-room he'd beat them savagely with rolled-up copies of *The Stage and Television Today* and curse them bitterly, leaving them without water and seeds for days on end. Remember, I'd been there for nearly a week and by that Thursday I knew pretty well the hatred that existed between him and his tiny troop of feathered Thespians.

His vilest humour he saved for Rajah, the biggest and strongest of the budgies. Rajah the Bengal Budgie finished the act off by riding a mono-cycle along a piece of string, four foot off the floor, carrying a pyramid of budgies piled on his outspread wings. Rudolpho hated him. He baited him with the end of his cigar when he came in drunk from the bar, singeing his tail feathers and laughing at him through the bars. 'You randy little Bengal beast,' he gibed, pointing to Aramintah, Rajah's mate. 'How you'd like to throw a leg across that, wouldn't you? Well, there's no chance, you're an absolute gherkin—you'll stay there like a feathered monk. No nookie for Rajah.'

And Rajah just shifted from claw to claw on his perch and snapped at Rudolpho with hate in his eyes, pacing the sanded floor of his cage, savagely

8

butting the plastic budgie on a spring on the end of his perch. 'You evil little git,' sneered Rudolpho, rattling the bars of Rajah's cage, 'You'd love to get at me wouldn't you? But you've got no chance.' And Rajah just looked through the bars at Rudolpho, loathing in his eyes, baring his beak.

'Leave him alone, you pitiless swine,' I said, making a movement towards him. But Rudolpho just laughed and slumped back on the sofa, a demijohn of cheap Somerset Port in his hand. I had half a mind to plant him one, there and then, but the concert secretary burst into the room to tell me that it was time for my second spot. He could see that something had been going on and looked quizzically at us for a minute, but his brain received the information and came out with its hands up.

'Time for your second spot,' he said, 'and if it's as good as your first I'm paying you off. You're as much use as a chocolate fire-guard.'

I turned and told Rudolpho, 'I'll sort you out later, you bastard.' Then I went on stage, not knowing that that was the last time that any of us would see him alive.

The last night of the week the club was fuller than usual. A gang of lads on a stag party had thrown up on the drummer and on the space invaders machine, fusing it. The evening hadn't even started yet—it was going to be lively. The floor was awash with beer and fag ends, and I could see that two of the lads on the stag night were only managing to stay upright because their mates had slipped their jackets over the backs of their chairs. The beer pumps were overheating and seizing up, and running the growing gauntlet of drunks were a dozen waitresses in Tyrolean blouses, the dark roots of their straw-coloured hair showing through, and their make-up flaking off like stucco from an old

Florentine palace. Gillette-mouthed and fast of elbow they cruised amongst the tables, strange galleons in a stranger sea, an increasing number of fiddled fivers being tucked into their bras and an ever-increasing number of thumb marks appearing on their bums.

I did my spot with as much inspiration and verve as a man cutting his toe-nails, picked on the minority groups like the Pakis and the Irish, and told a string of blue gags that were about as subtle as leprosy. Somebody started to heckle me and my timing went completely. Sweat broke out on my top lip, my legs turned to jelly and started shaking—I must have looked as though I was having a knee-tremble on my own. I attempted a joke about a Pakistani but gave him an Irish accent and completely lost the punch line, so I tried to ad lib about the state of the club. 'It'll be all right when it's finished. It's the first time I've worked in a morgue. Did they rent you lot from Tussaud's? Why don't you join hands and communicate with the living? Have you been drinking cement? I've seen more life in a dog's pelt.'

The audience just stared at me, with hate in their eyes. They didn't think it was funny, and neither did I. In the end I cued Los Geriatricos on the organ and drums and sang a couple of verses of 'I Want to be Happy', before lurching off the stage to an enthusiastic burst of apathy. Well, this is it, I thought. I've been going downhill faster than a runaway milk cart. I've been paid off from a lot of clubs, but this has got to be the worst. It's like a day-glo toilet. The concert secretary was already at the back of the stage waiting for me, and he looked like a one-man lynch mob. He opened his mouth and his few remaining teeth hung down slackly like an Australian Stonehenge. 'I don't know how you have the bleeding cheek to stand on a stage, you. I've seen better turns on the A1. If you're funny, I'll show my bum in the Vatican.'

'I don't need a bleeding part-timer to tell me how to do my act,' I grunted. 'Get stuffed.' I pushed open the dressing-room door. He followed me in, about to tell me I was as much use as a concrete parachute or a pork pie at a barmitzvah, when what we both saw shut us up completely.

The dressing-room looked as though someone had been rehearsing World War Three in it. All the budgies' cages had been torn apart and the birds were gone. The mirror was in splinters, the furniture smashed, the props were all over the floor and the make-up was smeared all over the walls. On the ceiling in Leichner number 4 a shaky hand had scrawled in bold capitals 'AND THE NUMBER OF THE BEAST IS 666' and below it 'THEN WORMS SHALL ALL HAVE EATEN THEE'. But in the centre of all this, like the still calm eye of a maelstrom, sprawled on the clapped-out settee, his head neatly severed from his body and placed in his lap, was Rudolpho the Great—a look of diabolical terror across what had once been his face.

I spent the next twenty-four hours in the police station, trying to explain how I couldn't have murdered him, wrecked the dressing-room, *and* done a twenty-minute comedy act at the same time.

'Yow were the last one with him and yow were the only one with a mowtive,' said the Detective Sergeant, a Brummie with hands like two pounds of badly-wrapped sausages. He looked as though he couldn't wait to make a necklace of them round my throat. 'Yow were heard to threaten him by the concert secretary, yow were,' he grunted through a face that was like a scale model of a disused claypits or the Schliemann diggings at Troy. I was just about to point out that I had left the dressing-room approximately 2.5 seconds after the concert secretary when a young constable opened the door of the interview room and said, 'Excuse me, sarge, can I have a quick word with you?' They stood together in a corner, and I caught a few words through the mutterings: 'Clawmarks, beaks, ribs, feathers in his mouth.' After a few minutes of this, the Sergeant came across to me again. His tone was that of a second-hand car salesman trying to get rid of a clapped-out Volkswagen Beetle that first saw action with Adolf Hitler and Eva Braun on the front seat. 'Ah well, Mr Burkitt, it looks as though yow've helped us as much as yow can. Thank yow for helping us with our enquiries and us'll be letting yow know if yow are needed again, yow.'

'It was Rajah, wasn't it?' I said, fixing the Sergeant with my eyes.

'What do yow mean?' he stuttered, the flab on his face twitching and reshaping itself into something like a nervous grin.

'Cut the flannel, Flatfoot,' I warbled as I lay back in the chair and lit a cigarette. 'You know I didn't do it, Seamus Smiles had buggered off home, there was nobody else back-stage but the budgies and there was nobody with a motive for killing Rudolpho but the budgies.' His mouth fell open. 'Leave off with the Mersey Tunnel impersonations,' I quipped, warming to the part. 'You'd better let me know what information you've got and I'll see if I can help you.'

It turned out that the police knew even less than I did. Rudolpho was a mystery to them as much as he was to me. Going through his personal belongings they'd found out only that he'd previously been employed as a male model in a catalogue of plumber's tools. I went home to my lodgings and had a night of troubled sleep, plagued with dreams of giant budgies with skinhead haircuts and Doc Martin boots on chasing me down endless concrete canyons and underpasses, reeking of urine and covered in aerosol graffiti, the doomed catacombs that the planners had turned the city' into. I staggered down to breakfast next morning and was about to launch a full frontal assault on my rancid kipper when I opened the newspaper and stopped in amazement, the fork suspended in mid-air.

The headlines said, 'Mass Killing Shock Outrage of Lonely Old Folk', while according to the text a wave of killings had taken place overnight, mainly along the south coast. There, in polite boarding-houses, in retirement bungalows and red-brick semis, in that world of chintz and Capo di Monte, ceramic shire-horses and souvenir spoon collec-tions, from Eastbourne to Hastings retired couples, spinster ladies and widows had been found cruelly savaged to death. The only apparent link in all the killings was an empty budgie cage swinging on its stand, its feathered denizens fled. After I'd put the newspaper down I phoned the Sergeant. His wife answered—sometimes life is like that.

'Where's Flatfoot?' I snarled down the phone.

'He's coming,' she breathed heavily back.

'I don't want to know about your sex life,' I quipped.

Flatfoot was worried. He'd seen the reports too.

'This thing's hotter than Beelzebub's bum,' I growled.

'What are we goin' to do?' he asked.

'Well, it's obvious that something's happening to the budgie population of this country, and that something isn't nice.'

14

'We ought to tell somebody, the Press or someone.'

'The Press,' I said. 'Don't tell anything to the Press. They could make yes sound like no. We've got to go right to the top.'

'Yow mean I should tell the Inspector?'

I'd met the Inspector the night before. He could put two and two together and make a camel. 'No,' I said, 'he's as bright as the inside of a hedgehog's bum. We've got to go right to the top with this one.'

'The Chayfe Constibul?'

I thought of that flat-capped moustachioed moron to the far right of Hermann Goering, his pig-like eyes searching for the Marxist in every traffic offender. The man who wanted to re-introduce transportation for being drunk and disorderly, and burning through the gristle of the nose for double parking. I saw him in my mind's eye, his double chins falling like a row of sofas beneath a mouth like the dried-up washer off a bike pump.

'No, this has got to go to London. Somehow we've got to see the PM. I'll see you by the left luggage office at Euston tomorrow noon.' I slammed the receiver down and walked out of the phone booth into a thick London fog, which was a bit unnerving since I was in Manchester at the time.

Next day I got the earliest train I could to London. It was the Pullman, the Executive Special, full of grey-suited men reading pink newspapers. Through my half-closed eyes, they blurred until they looked like a herd of donkeys making love to flamingoes in an African salt-pan; a fanciful thought that impressed no one, not even myself. I watched them for a while—those smug, bloated, crass, ignorant fools—amazed that they could be so blindly unaware that all our lives were about to be changed

irreversibly. I thought of some lines of the Zen
Buddhist poet, Yen Sing:

'The wind blows in the night
By my window the peach tree shakes
I sit before the fire and roast my nuts
Ayee! Ayee!'

How fitting, I thought, though to what I didn't know.
The train rattled on and I studied the men around me
carefully. They were of two types. The self-made and
struggling young executives with Morocco leather
briefcases and Rolex Oyster watches were going to
London to sell advertising, property, computers and
double-glazing, to meetings, expense account
lunches, suites in top-class hotels, and expensive
dinners followed by large glasses of Rémy and a visit
from the Little Sisters of the Rich Visiting Massage
Service. They were the men who kept Britain's
economy churning sluggishly towards the cliff edge.
The others were the men with the public school haircuts, the senior civil servants, the heads of our public
industries, the Rotary Club and Masonic Mafia, all
bulging waistcoats and necks. One fat senior
specimen, with half-moon glasses, was reading *The
Grocer*; others were braying in loud voices, calling
out letters of the alphabet linked with verbs and
splattered with figures.

'BG said that TC had given out GKN's closing offer at
2.4 plus annual ZPR's. PP told me that GM had leaked it
to FT that 2.4 was at least one below the GNP. Then
again, he always was a little turd.'

How little you know, you empty men, I thought. As
you lie by the sides of your equine or bovine wives
tonight in Richmond and Twickenham, Chingford
and Reading, how little you know that forces that
you'll never dream of are stalking the face of the

16

earth, red in beak and claw, and that some rough beast, its time come again, slouches towards Billericay to be reborn.

In the dining car one of the grey-suited, pink-papered grey people ordered a kipper and soused it with Worcester Sauce and at that precise moment a baby executive, cultivating his first ulcer like a rare pearl, looked up from his cardboard bacon and exclaimed loudly, 'Ye Gods!' I followed his gaze out across the flickering turnip fields and the Ovaltine Farm. On the horizon a monstrous black cloud, like a venomous billowing serpent spewing Stygian bile across the skies above Leighton Buzzard, was advancing towards us in overdone prose. As it got closer it filled the sky above us, blotting out the sun.

'They must be locusts,' shouted one of the men.

'Locusts in England?' someone else yelled. 'Never! They're migrating earwigs or something. I read something in *The Times* about them last year. It was ladybirds or earwigs or something of the sort. Supposed to be a lot of them, anyway. Played the devil with the roses and, em, the delphiniums, don't you know.'

'In January?' somebody said, 'You don't get ladybirds in January.'

'They're budgies,' I told them coolly.

'Budgies!' they laughed at me superciliously.

'Budgies,' I said, repeating myself vehemently.

'Impossible!' cried the men amazedly.

'On the contrary it's possible, probable and definite,' I replied authoritatively.

Then, just as we were about to run out of adverbs, the train gave a lurch and slammed to a halt, throwing kippers into the lap of the grocer and covering a lot of baby executives with scrambled eggs, Lea and Perrin's sauce and Cooper's Oxford marmalade. Ahead of us the track was completely blocked by a pile of tree trunks and the engine of the train had been completely skewed on its side so that its wheels revolved uselessly as diesel fumes and smoke filled the air. Men jumped from carriages in raw panic and ran across the fields as the sky above them darkened with a mass of beating wings. The move proved to be a foolish one, for the budgies—swooping low—chased them across the ploughed furrows. I watched as a terrified bureaucrat was lifted bodily a hundred foot into the air and dropped on to an escaping systems analyst and the director of a firm with interests in strip mining, video rentals, quick food restaurant chains, instant potatoes, and cable TV. They were all killed outright.

'Perhaps,' I thought to myself, 'the birds aren't all that bad'.

The train looked like a Manchester United football special after an away game with the Ghenghis Khan eleven, bodies were strewn everywhere, most of them covered in British Rail gravy. The dead were the lucky ones. Those who survived would never get rid of the smell—like lepers they'd wander for the rest of their natural chuffs, shunned by mortal men, condemned like the Ancient Mariner to stop people on their way home from weddings and tell them the story of how their lives were blighted for ever by British Rail gravy.

I jumped down from the train. For the moment the birds had gone. Dying ex-public schoolboys, their Papermate pens stuck through their chests, were screaming for matron. I walked down the line to where the engine lay on its side; nearby the driver was sitting on a rock, his head in his hands. (Fortunately it was still attached to his body.)

'What happened?' I asked.

'The budgies,' he croaked. 'They just picked the train up and turned it over.'

'How?'

'I slowed down because of that tree across the rails, and they flew down at us. There were just so many of them—they all grabbed hold of a bit and flapped . . . and bang, wallop, we were off the track, guv'nor.'

I had to think hard. Why this train? What were they after? Like a slowly gathering boil, like spilt tea soaking into a tablecloth, like steam rising off porridge, the idea slowly got through. They were after me! They were obviously trying to stop me getting to London! I looked at the driver—he was about my size.

'Change clothes with me,' I said.

'What for?' he asked.

I shoved five loaded twenty pound notes under his nose.

'I've always wanted a candy striped suit with day-glo cowboy boots,' he told me, ripping off his jacket.

We changed clothes quickly and I hurried off across the fields. As I scrambled through a hawthorn hedge I heard a diabolical scream. Looking back I saw a man in a candy-striped suit and day-glo cowboy boots being chased across the hills by a thickening cloud of budgies. He never made it to safety—there was another scream, and he was lifted bodily into the air and carried northwards.

'Poor swine,' I said to myself, chuckling.

Half an hour's walk took me to the outskirts of a village. I looked at my reflection in a puddle. It was muddy. No more cigarettes and whisky for me, I thought, it's jogging, Perrier water, muesli and women with flat sandals, plaits, moustaches and no bras from now on. A sign announced that here was Much Hadham Village, twinned with Merdeville, France. A hundred yards away, parked in front of what looked like the village hall, was an old green Morris van circa 1956. The village dozed in the warmth of an English summer's day—which was strange because it was late January. Cats basked on the roadside in dark glasses reading the *Sunday Telegraph*. Bees hummed, and those that knew the words sang. Outside the village pub that carried on its signboard a picture of a horned man and the name the Merry Cuckold, some old men dozed in the heat, their ale in tankards at their feet: old men doddery and rusty in the twilight of their days, covered in cobwebs and suspicious stains. I looked about—apart from the old geezers the place was deserted. Then I heard a noise. Four women came out of the village hall carrying a large pot of something steaming that smelt of monosodium glutamate and charity.

The WVS!

I sprinted over, there was hope for England yet! 'Ladies,' I blurted out, 'You've got to do as I say!'

They almost dropped their reeking burden.

'Oh,' cried one of them, the largest of the four, built like a mattress filled with cabbages and with the protuberant teeth and vanishing chin of the Home Counties middle class. She looked like a coypu in

Jaeger. 'Don't worry, gels,' she squealed, looking straight at me. 'I know how to handle this. Stand back you—you—you man, you.' She looked me up and down, her nose wrinkled in disgust: I felt like something a dog had done on her best rug. 'He's either a rapist or a madman or both, girls. Leave this to me.'

At that moment the badly-fitting trousers of the railwayman fell to the ground exposing my Y-fronts to their not uninterested gaze. I had forgotten that, for safety's sake, I had shoved a large roll of money in tens and fives down the front of my underpants, when I changed clothes with the train driver. The result was that I seemed to be sporting what, in the Army, would have been called a kidney-swiper but is known in politer circles as a dinger of a donger.

'I knew it! He's a crazed sex-fiend!' shrieked this Brunhilde of the Bath buns as my trousers fell.

'Now, Leonie, don't be too hasty. The poor boy looks frightened,' another one said soothingly. She was very tall and thin, with bright red hair, and was standing next to a little dark-haired lady with eyes like pools of treacle and busts so large she wasn't on speaking terms with her feet.

'I need your help, ladies. I'm on my way to serve the Prime Minister.'

'No wonder she always looks happy,' said the red-haired gel, looking at my well-filled jocks and nodding like a matchstick with a loose head.

The women put down their hot nutritious soup and advanced towards me. 'The old people, the meals on wheels,' I cried tremulously.

'Let them eat coke,' said a little one with a squint so bad that whenever she looked at me I looked over both my shoulders to see if somebody was behind me. They lunged and grabbed me. Lips met and were pressed together feverishly, madly smacking at each other like epileptic limpets. They smacked and sucked and sucked and smacked like rampant sink plungers. In what seemed seconds my clothes were off, their clothes were off, and we were all off. Buttocks were squeezed, thighs were stroked, breasts were kissed. I lined them up like whippets at a starting gate and pleasured them 'au façon de doggie' as the French say. I worked my way along taking them one at a time like a riveter working his way along an oil tanker. We tried every position in the book, then we ad libbed and threw the book out of the window, or at least would have done if there'd been a window handy.

'Scrum down,' shouted the red-haired gel. And scrum down we did. Sometimes they were on top, sometimes I was on top; it looked like 'hunt the thimble' in an artificial limb store. Sometimes nobody was on top, but that was only when we stopped at half-time to suck lemons. Then lemon went home and we started again.

All through that unforgettable day, as an August sun burned in a January sky, we sported on the grass, I and the four insatiable daughters of the Blue Rinse and Twin Set Brigade. They were past their first youthful flush, but made up in determination, numbers and pack formation what they lacked in years.

We went through every permutation possible with five sets of limbs. At one time I was pushing so hard I ploughed a furrow up the field with the red-head's nose and banged the google-eyed one's head against a tree, straightening her eyes out. Unfortunately, her ears went askew so that she looked as though her head was cocked quizzically to one side.

At last I collapsed, exhausted. 'Ladies, enough of this jollity,' I cried. 'I'm on a serious mission, you must help me.'

I explained my errand to them and ten minutes later we were dressed and lurching in the meals on wheels van past the Merry Cuckold towards London. I nodded towards the wizened grey-haired creatures, toothless and rheumy-eyed, that were dribbling down their chins outside the pub.

'Game old cocks,' I quipped.

'Not at all,' snorted Brunhilde. 'They're only seventeen, came here on a YOP scheme. Just can't stand the pace, that's all. I don't know what's happening to men nowadays.'

I looked at the dried-up seventeen-year-old creatures slobbering and drooling their gummy way towards the big nothing, and thanked the Lord I was leaving Much Hadham.

Three days later, after stopping in every lay-by and patch of common land for repeat performances, I kissed them goodbye outside Euston Station. I was two stone lighter, my hair greying at the temples and my nether regions twitching like a diviner's rod in a swamp. Flatfoot was already there. In fact the poor devil had been there for three days.

'Where've yow bin?' he asked, his lower lip trembling. 'Oi've bin here for three days. Yow promised yow'd be 'ere and yow weren't. Oi 'avn't even 'ad an oice lolly.'

'The train went off the rails, you must have heard.'

'Oh ahr. Oi thort eet sed "went off to Wales",' he cried, a glimmer of unintelligent thought burning at the back of his mind like a workman's brazier at the end of a long foggy tunnel. He had a brain like Shrewsbury, nothing much happened there.

'Now we can't waste any more time, we've got to see the PM. But first some oysters, brown ale, glucose tablets and raw meat, I've had a long ride.'

As we ate in a chophouse by the Thames at Wapping, Flatfoot told me how in the last few days more and more people had been found dead along the south coast. It seemed as though the death of Rudolpho the Great had suddenly sparked off a wave of budgie-owner killings that seemed as senseless as it was inexplicable. When we arrived at the door of Number 10, a policeman with a broken nose and eyes like cigarette burns in a blanket was stamping his feet together on the doorstep in a vain attempt to drive some of the blood back into his brains. He should have succeeded, really, since it only had to reach his bum.

'We've got to see the Prime Minister,' we told the policeman.

'You got an appointment, sir?' he burbled superciliously through lips like mating sausages.

'No, not really, but we've got to see her. It's a matter of the utmost importance.'

Then with a flourish that surprised me, Flatfoot produced his CID card.

'Very interesting, sir, but I wouldn't care if you were Fabian of the Yard or Starsky and Hutch. You can't come in here without an appointment. I'm only doing my job, sir. Don't make it difficult for me.'

'Look, I'm desperate, can't you let us in?' I said. 'We want to talk to her about the budgies.'

'Look, sir, it's more than my job's worth and, if I may say so, the Prime Minister has more to do than talk about birds with a railwayman who is obviously in a state of sexual excitement. She has trivial things to do like running the country and fighting wars.'

'Sexual excitement?' I asked. I looked down. 'That's my money,' I said. 'And what we're talking about is a matter of national importance, these budgies are dangerous.'

'All budgies are if swallowed,' he quipped and started to chuckle. When a policeman chuckles it starts at his boots. So rare is it that he ever says anything funny that it takes a while to work its way up to his throat and it sounds for all the world rather like somebody regurgitating ball-bearings.

In this case the laughter began rhythmically as a low booming sound, like someone tapping the side of an empty gasometer with a large Bavarian Bierwurst, then it worked its way up until it sounded like a wheezy pump in poor mechanical order shifting slurry from one sewage pond to another. He doubled up with mirth at his own jest. I tried to ignore him.

'Look,' I said, 'my name's Eric Chuckles—a laugh, a song and a balloon.' I gave him my card.

'Might come in handy for the policemen's children's Christmas party this year,' he spluttered, wiping tears of merriment from his eyes. 'Do you do kids do's? Old MacDonald's Farm, blowing the balloons up and tying them into dogs and all that?'

I ignored him. Flatfoot grunted.

'Listen yow, we're goin' to stay at the Ritz Hotel. Yow'd better let her 'ighness know, orl roit. Just tell 'er we know orl about the budgies, orl roit.'

We booked into the Islington Ritz, a one-star doss house mentioned in the Egon Ronay Good Flatulence Guide, where the bedbugs were queueing up to see what room we booked into. The landlady had been drummed out of the Mafia for cruelty. She stood at the door, eyes like hypodermics and a face like an ironing board, a beardless Ayatollah. 'No coloureds, no Irish and no women in your room. Breakfast at eight thirty sharp, no singing, no unnecessary smiling. Here's your soap.' She handed over a piece of soap that could have got lost under your toenails, then disappeared. I had a shower in water that was hot and rust-coloured and then we turned on the gas-powered TV. It wasn't even black and white, only grey and grey. We were just in time for the news, and what we heard stopped us in our tracks.

'This is Dobbin Ray, London. An unexplained spate of deaths that has taken place over the last three days along the south coast seems to have spread northwards to encompass all regions of the country. From Inverness to Eastbourne, old ladies have been found savagely mutilated, the only common factor an empty budgie's cage. Police, believing this to be the work of experienced and highly-organized budgie rustlers, have posted men at airports and docks looking for suspects with small perforated suitcases. However, following the derailment of a train three days ago, and the pecking to death of several policemen in the North, the search has been called off and experts are now beginning to consider that the killings may be the work of a highly-trained force of savage birds. It is not known yet whether the birds are Soviet-trained. The Prime Minister has refused to comment, and the Foreign Secretary said that Argentinian involvement has not been ruled out. Dominic Selfridge went this afternoon to the London University School of Zoology to talk to the head of the ornithology department, Professor I. C. Clearenough.'

Selfridge's face came on the screen. 'Professor,' his oily tones flowed, 'do you believe there is any truth in the rumour that these killings are being carried out by a flock of highly-trained budgies?'

The professor smiled as though he was talking to a simpleton, which in fact he was. 'None at all, none at all, absolute nonsense. For budgies to derail a train they would have to be seventy feet tall, seventy feet tall. As far as the killings are concerned—well, budgies, as we all know, are dear little creatures, dear little creatures.' (This man had his own built-in echo system.) 'We have many in our aviary here, and most of them have been bred in captivity. I mean just look at them, look at them.' He turned to point at the cage behind him, full of yellow and green and blue and grey speckled creatures. 'Would any man expect those pretty little things, *parakeetus parakeeti*, to have any violent feelings at all? Nonsense, nonsense.' He turned again. 'Good God,' he muttered.

The image on the screen shifted slightly.

Someone had obviously jogged the cameraman. It blurred a little, then settled again. What we saw was amazing: the budgies *en masse*, driven by some force beyond themselves, were bunched and straining at the bars of their cage. A very powerful bird forced his wings through the bars and with other budgies round him helping, pulled and strained and struggled until the cage buckled before our eyes. The budgies zoomed out of the cage in a riot of colour and noise and the picture blurred again. Just before the camera crashed to the floor and the screen went blank, we heard a hellish scream—it was as though a fiend from the infernal regions had risen through the floor of the ornithological department of the London University School of Zoology—and saw the professor slump to the ground, his jugular vein pumping claret like an Arab's oilwell. The last words we heard before the screen went blank were, 'Dominic Selfridge, News at Ten, London Uniarg, grooch, splurg, morg.'

Flatfoot and I looked at each other. The phone rang, I answered it; sometimes life's like that. A voice said, 'This is 10 Downing Street here. Am I talking to Mr Chuckles, Mr Eric Chuckles—a smile, a song and a balloon?'

'Yes,' I said. 'What do you want?'

'The Prime Minister wants you to come round here right away. Take a cab and be here as soon as you can.'

Half an hour later Flatfoot and I walked up to the door of Number 10. The same policeman nodded us in. We walked through the door into the Prime Minister's personal appartments, leaving the policeman spitting teeth out on to the pavement like a man choking on mints.

'He fell on me boot, loike,' said Flatfoot.

The Prime Minister looked up from the table as we

entered. She was taller than I'd thought, heftier too. She looked like a bouncer for the Women's Institute with her permed hair flying up in a wave like the prow of a helmet, her eyes fierce and staring like those of an inquisitional monk, and her mouth set and hard like a pink steam-hammer. When she smiled, it was as though an eskimo had appeared on a Mediterranean beach towing an ice floe behind him. She had the nullified face of a professional politician or a mass murderer. She shifted a plug of tobacco from one cheek to the other, and spat a thin stream of yellow juice into the fire as she took my hand and crushed it within hers. She was crunching bones in my hand that didn't even know that they were bones. When she spoke, still holding my hand in a vice-like grip, it was in a voice that sounded like somebody tipping coke.

'We checked you out, Chuckles. You're clean. Not much of a comic, but you're clean.'

'I've never been a clean comic,' I quipped. Her grip tightened, sending globs of pain shooting up the veins of my arm, knocking at the doors of my brain. I tried not to let them in, but they had the key. They let themselves in and rearranged my features into a twisted smile.

'Not clean like that,' she snarled. 'Clean for us. You're British, white and have been a boy scout. You've never been a member of any illegal organization or read the *Guardian* or *New Statesman* or made fun of Conservative women's hats. To us, that means clean.' She let go of my hand, and the blood shot down it, filling my squeezed-out flesh like a foot being thrust into a sock.

'Sit down,' she cracked out. 'Now, before you tell us what you know, tell us what you know.'

I deduced that this was typical politician's jargonese and told her all about Rajah and Rudolpho and his Performing Budgies.

'Fudge,' she said angrily when I'd finished. She spat in the fire. 'It's the Commies, I knew they were in it.' At that moment her husband stuck his head round the door. He was a thin cadaverous man, with sparse grey hair streaked across his head, and rheumy eyes peering through thick wire-rimmed glasses like Siamese whelks. A copy of *Lives of the Great Poisoners* was under his arm.

'Darling, dearest chuck. May I go out now for a few wets with the chaps?'

'No, you can get back into your room and clean it up. You were naughty yesterday and you must be punished. You can't go out until you've finished tidying your room, and I want every speck of dust cleaned up. We can't have everyone doing what they want. I'm the only one allowed to do that.'

He slunk out. I back-tracked a paragraph.

'Commies?' I asked. 'Reds under the bed?'

'Reds,' she spat. 'Subversive, destructive socialists, morons, nationalizers, destroyers of all that we held dear in the 1930s, the golden age of England.'

'The Thirties? The Jarrow hunger march, poverty, ill health, black-shirted fascists walking the streets, disastrous slums in every city, millions living below the breadline, massive unemployment and inequality?'

'Precisely. You must remember' (and a soft, hypnotic, we-are-all-reasonable-people-here quality came into her voice), 'poverty and inequality are an Englishman's birthright. These murders of innocent old ladies, the old and the infirm, are the work of Trotskyite cells. Someone has trained those budgies. Somebody big. We think it's a mole.'

'A mole?' said Flatfoot, who'd been so overawed at meeting his country's leader that he'd been struck dumb for several minutes. 'Em, er—excuse me, your highness—but er, yow now—em, how can a mole train—er—budgies, like, yow?'

The Prime Minister flung herself down on the settee and crossed her legs. I hadn't realized she was a Catholic.

'As of yet we're not really sure. Okay, so, Chuckles tell us what you know.'

'I know he tormented Rajah. That's all I know. He deserved what he got.'

'So why the mass killings? Why the old ladies in Bexhill and Poole? Why the message on the ceiling, six six six and all that, and the bit about the worms?'

'I don't know.'

'We're trying to crack the code at the moment. Some of our best brains are working on it, every computer in the country is working on it. But I'll tell you, in the mean time, what we do know. Rudolpho's real name was Ernie Blighton. He was a fellow traveller of Philby, Blunt, Burgess and MacLean. The Red Toga Tuggers of Cambridge, the Scarlet Turd Burglars.'

My mouth fell open.

She smiled for the first time and filled her pipe again with the morass of black shag that she'd been rolling between her palms. 'He'd been working for the Russians for years, and when he went down from Cambridge he got a job in the Ministry of Defence. All the time he was passing on information through a plant in Hyde Park.'

'A plant?'

'He used to go and talk to a rhododendron bush. People thought he was mad. "There's Ernie talking to the bushes again," they used to say. What they didn't know was that a microphone in the bushes was connected straight to the Russian Embassy.'

'The swine! The diabolical fiends!' I shuddered

32

and sat down.

'What did he get out of this?'

'Free tickets for the Bolshoi Ballet.'

'What?'

'He just loved those young Russian men jumping about in tights looking as if they've got five pounds of badly-wrapped fruit down the front of their jock-straps.'

'Where do the budgies come into it? Why Rudolpho the Great?'

'That was a respectable front. After he left the MOD he worked for M15, MFI, BOC, BICC, the RSPCA and then he went to ground. Our man was after him by then. We'd put Smiley on to the job, then we put Dopey, Sneezy, Happy, Grumpy and finally Snow White.'

'Snow White!'

'The greatest secret agentess the world has ever known, so secret she didn't know who she was herself until last year.'

'Who is she?'

'Her name was Griselda Marrowfat. To all intents and purposes she was just an ordinary housewife, married to the night watchman of a government cat's-eye warehouse in Dorking. She infiltrated the Ring. But the trouble was he knew that she knew.'

'She knew he knew she knew.'

'He knew she knew that he knew she knew.'

'What happened?'

'Nobody knows. The next thing we knew, old ladies all over England are dying and the terrible thing is we can't blame it on the Labour Party or the unions. If only we could pin it on them. Oh, it makes me want to vomit.'

Her husband looked round the door. 'Er, gin and tonic? Yes, please dear.'

She flung a perfectly-aimed chair at him, a leg of which caught him between the eyes and dropped him to the ground, frothing at the mouth. She ignored him.

'Look, quite simply the facts are these. Somehow the budgies are gathering, communicating, swelling in numbers, setting themselves free. It's a sort of feathered socialism.' She shuddered as she said the words. 'The only thing we know is that it all began with the escape of this one called Roger.'

'Rajah,' I corrected.

'From now on, we will call him Roger,' she corrected, looking at me sternly with eyes like blazing chip-pans in a coal cellar. 'You will go back to your hotel now and sleep, and tomorrow we will meet again to discuss it.'

She dismissed us with a wave of her hand, and relit her pipe.

We stepped over the slumped frame of her husband. He whispered goodnight from his pool of blood as we closed the door gently behind us.

The next morning we awoke at seven. Flatfoot went down to try and get some breakfast. The dining room was empty so he went into the kitchen. That was deserted too save for an empty budgie cage and the landlady's body slumped in a chair. Flatfoot came back with all he could find, a tin of dog food and some dog biscuits, and started eating them cold with a spoon. He offered me some, but I refused. As things turned out later, it was lucky I did so. He finished the tin and rubbed his belly in a satisfied fashion, burping loudly.

'Yow won't believe what's happened down there.' He nodded towards the floor. 'The owd bugger's dead. Well, eet just serves her roit, 'er an' 'er no bluddy singin'.' He grinned to himself. 'Oi sang three verses of "Una Paloma Blanca" just tew get me own back. Roit in 'er bluddy ear!!'

I turned the radio on to hear Terry Wogan back-announcing a Dolly Parton record.

'Well there you are then, and what a way to start the day. There she is, what a fine lump of woman she is. The best little lunghouse in Texas. Oh now, would you look at this. It's an epistle or two, a missive from the DG, and I thought he'd forgotten me entirely. After our last little tiff. We had words, you see, about his dog, but now somebody's just pushed this piece of paper in front of me nose, with writing on it, and it's joined-up writing as well. There's clever for you. Maybe it isn't the DG, I don't think he can write. Or maybe again it could be his writing, it looks like a spider's crawled all over the page. Now, what's all this then? Oh, the newsroom has some news for you. I hope it's not trivial. So over we go now to the newsroom.'

An announcer, in a voice that cracked with emotion, said, 'We interrupt this programme to bring you a special announcement. Air traffic control at Heathrow Airport and the RAF early warning system at Shepherd's Bush last night discovered a massive flock of what seems to be birds winging their way towards London. As many as two hundred million birds are thought to be moving towards the capital in a cloud four miles long and two miles wide. All air traffic has been grounded after six Harrier jump jets sent up from RAF Brize Norton were brought down by the birds. Although reports are rather confused at the moment, it seems that a special squad of kamikaze budgies with iridium-tipped beaks were responsible. The Royal Family were evacuated from London and left for Balmoral this morning aboard a special train. The Prime Minister is at this moment still in the House of Commons after an all-night sitting—it is expected that she will make a statement on behalf of the government. Jonathan Bumblebee is on the spot in Whitehall.'

The broadcast went over, live, to the Houses of Parliament. Jonathan Bumblebee spoke in an urgent and concerned voice. 'The Prime Minister is about to speak at this moment. The House is hushed, a tremendous sense of history in the making permeates the air. A sense of destiny, a feeling of such vital significance that only a mere two dozen or so of the MPS who've been here all night are asleep. And now the PM is walking towards the dispatch box, the venerable walls of this historic building are echoing with the quiet murmur of expectant conversation.'

'Mr Speaker and honourable members,' she began, her voice echoing about the vaults of the mother of parliaments like a tin can falling down a flight of stairs. A lone Home Counties waffler with a sense of the historic shouted, 'Speak for England, thingy.' A cacophony of 'Hear, hears' almost drowned out her next words. Honourable members, it is my unfortunate duty to tell this House that London is in the gravest peril.'

The MP for somewhere in Essex shouted, 'Shame,' and fell asleep again. The Prime Minister continued. 'For some time past we in the Cabinet have been aware of forces at work in this country, determined to undermine our way of life, determined to force the people of this island sanctuary of ours to relinquish the freedom which has for hundreds of years been our heritage, our father's heritage, and that of their father's before them and so on and so forth. Never in the history of our island race has so much been done in so long a time and in so many ways. In fact, as it were, this of course we hold to be so, to be our God-given destiny.' (*Groans, hear-hears, cheers, mooing noises, shouts of, 'Get on with it you silly old bat' 'Roll on demob,' etc.*) 'This very morning, however, I heard from the Ministry of Defence that a massive flock of deranged and evil budgies—'(*Gasps, bursts of laughter, calls of 'Rubbish', and 'Keep on with the tweetment' and shouts from the Speaker of 'Order, order'.*) 'Coming from we know not where but no doubt trained and supported by forces out to disrupt our way of life.' (*Groans, 'Reds under the beds', shouts for order.*) 'The Ministry of Defence tells me that the birds are well organized and well equipped and that attempts to destroy them by military means have failed. It is my grave duty to inform you that the wossname, the RAF, have lost a hundred and twenty-six planes and sixteen helicopters and the Army have lost a number of anti-missile launches and their men.' (*Cries of 'Shame', 'Resign', uproar generally, shouts of 'Order, order'.*) 'This is an open and unprovoked act of aggression and an infringement of our sovereignty. In accordance with the powers invested in me, I have no alternative but to declare a state of national emergency.' (*Uproar, shouts.*)

The voice of Jonathan Bumblebee intruded. 'Well, the Prime Minister has just sat down after uttering some of the most amazing words this House has ever heard. And now the Leader of the Opposition is walking towards the dispatch box.'

The hubbub died down and the Leader of the Opposition spoke in a tremulous voice. 'Would the Honourable Lady care to tell the House firstly how her government could have been so blindly oblivious to this so-called invasion for so long, and can she also tell this House secondly at what hour these budgies are expected to arrive in London and thirdly what their intentions will be when they get here.' (*Shouts of 'Sit down!' 'Traitor!' 'Quisling!' 'Four-eyed prune!'*)

The PM got up again. 'The Honourable Gentleman— who seems to be lacking in any sense of patriotism or honour—asked me how long ago we were aware of the danger of invasion. Well, that is

37

something I am not prepared to comment upon at this moment. Our Intelligence reports suggested a build-up of birds, but we were not entirely convinced that they would be so foolhardy as to attempt an open and illegal act of armed aggression against our sovereignty.' (*Cries from the opposition of 'Rubbish', 'Get stuffed!' 'Nonsense!' 'Shove your head in a bucket!'*) 'To the second question I would reply that the expected time of arrival is two pm Greenwich mean time, and the answer to the third question is that I believe their purpose to be the total destruction of our freedom and our way of life as we know it.'

There was an explosion of shouting, booing, hissing and general noise that sounded like a herd of rutting armadillos making love to rubber donkeys in a lake of tapioca pudding. There were groans and yells, shouts and what sounded like fists smacking heads until the Speaker restored order again.

Then the MP for Little Gidding got up and asked if budgies could commit rape. Somebody else shouted 'Only with other budgies.' (*General laughter.*)

The Honourable Member for East Coker asked if the budgies thought they would be allowed to carry on like this in Russia. Then he was butted in the face by a left-wing MP from the Welsh mining valleys. Just before the broadcast went off the air several MPS shouted that it was a communist plot and an MP for a Scottish Highlands constituency said that the Highland regiments should be issued with guards to prevent budgies from flying up their kilts. The MP for Burnt Norton asked if the ratepayer was going to be asked once again to foot the bill for all this disruption. The broadcast went off the air and Terry Wogan came back on.

'Well, there you go. It never rains but it pours and I

thought budgies were such nice little homely things. What do you think, Eric?'

Eric Mindrot, the DJ of the programme about to follow, muttered a few sycophantic things about the Prime Minister before we switched off, nauseated by his treacly whine.

Flatfoot grunted. 'Well, the sheet's rayly heet the fan now. Yow know, it looks loike London's rayly in for eet.'

We were interrupted by a knocking at the door. I opened the door: attached to the knock was a fist, on the end of which was a small mountain shaped like a Special Branch man. 'The PM wants you both right away,' he muttered through lips like cuts in a blancmange.

Ten minutes later were were speeding through the streets in an official car. Police outriders cleared the way for us. There was an unusual number of people on the streets, all moving in the same direction— away.

'Where are they all going?' I asked the Special Branch officer.

'They're clearing out,' he grunted. 'Panic's starting to spread. That's what comes of informing the public. They ought to have been kept in the dark.'

'Do yow now, Oi keep theenking I'm a dog.' Flatfoot volunteered this information apropos of nothing.

'Are you serious?' I asked Flatfoot, hardly expecting his dull imagination to have invented anything like that as a joke.

'Yees, it's trew. For the last arf 'our Oi've been feelin' rayle funny. Oi keep wanting tew bark and chase cats and roger people's legs and such loike.'

'Is he barmy?' the Special Branch man asked.

'I don't think so,' I replied. 'He ate a tin of dog food this morning and that could explain it. Just before you came, he nearly put his back out trying to lick his town halls. I'd wondered what he was trying to do.'

As we sped down Mornington Crescent I noticed a crowd of people chanting and singing and dancing at the side of the road. 'Who are they?' I asked.

'Religious freaks,' muttered Special Branch. 'It's some flat-earth "God was a spaceman" cult welcoming the end of the world or something.'

I wound down the windows as we approached the group. There must have been two or three hundred of them, dressed in white smocks, sandals and carrying placards saying: 'God will not be mocked', 'Let loose the budgies of war' and 'Vengeance is mine saith the Lord.'

Someone who had obviously lost his way amongst them was carrying a board that said 'Mamma's pizzeria and spaghetti house for the best pizza in town'. He went down in a welter of flailing cards and boots, his cries for help drowned in the massed voices singing the tune of 'John Brown's Body', but the words weren't any I'd heard before.

> *See the budgies they are coming through the sky*
> *To bring the wrath of God and deliver us on high*
> *In their feathered glory we will fly to paradise*
> *Oh praise, oh praise the budgies*
> *Glory, glory to the budgies*
> *Glory, glory to the budgies...'*

I wound up the windows, nauseated. How could they believe such rubbish? Flatfoot coughed. 'Erm, do yow think yow could feel moy nose and feel if it's wet, loike, only I don't feel tew good.'

I felt his nose, it was dry and hot. His coat looked dull and lacklustre too. 'I'll get you a bowl of water and some conditioning powders when we get to Downing Street.'

He looked happier at that. If he'd had a tail he'd have wagged it.

The car spun round the corner, only to find the way ahead blocked by a surging tide of humanity. Thousands of people clutching bundles of possessions were jamming the streets, their eyes glazed and mad with grief and woe. It looked like a dress rehearsal for Doomsday, humanity to the welter in despair, like going-home time at Cardiff Arms Park after Wales has been beaten by England. A police outrider came back towards us.

'It's no use, sir, we can't get through, the streets are blocked all round. We've radioed ahead but there's no one answering at Traffic. I think they've buggered off, too.'

The Special Branch man cursed. 'It's no good,' he said. 'We'll have to get there on foot.'

He leapt from the car. We followed, pushing ourselves into the crowd in his wake, buffeting against the flow of bodies. For a few minutes we kept together, then I found myself being hustled and dragged off course in this river of fear. I lost sight of the man from Special Branch and the last time I saw Flatfoot as I was bundled along with the tide of humanity he was fighting with a poodle in a shop doorway over a bone. I tried to push against the crowd but it was useless. I struggled to free my arm. I looked at my watch. One thirty, only half an hour to go. Suddenly the sky turned black, darkness fell, a million faces looked up, a million voices cried out. Above, earlier than expected, were the budgies, their whirring wings and maniacal cheeping making a mind-shattering roar.

'Cheeky Joey, cheeky Joey, cheeky Joey,' cheeped two million beaks in unison, as the streets were covered with darkness. People all around screamed and panicked, running madly in every direction. I managed to punch and kick my way into a shop doorway as the crowd went berserk with fear.

Echelons of birds detached themselves from the main body and dropped to earth, only to rise again carrying men and women bodily upwards. Then they dropped them from a great height on to the people below. I remembered the train crash. The fiends! The budgies had invented the person bomb.

I leaned against the shop door in terror. It gave way, opening inwards. I fell in and found myself in the dimly-lit interior of a high class ladies' milliners. I shut the door behind me and looked around. Here at least was safe refuge for a while. Then a voice from the darkness said softly. 'Lock the door, sweetheart, we don't want to be disturbed, do we?'

I did as I was told—that voice could have been on the end of a gun for all I knew. Then, from the shadows at the rear of the shop, she came forward, dressed in the thinnest of gold sheath dresses, her bright red hair falling in rivers of sunset hue on to her creamy shoulders. Her dress, split to the top of her thighs, showed long sleek legs with just a hint of stocking top. Her face was the face of a woman barely concealing underneath her smile the raging lusts of an animal, such as a hamster or a gerbil. Her heaving breasts straining against the thin shimmering material looked like bald wrestler's heads with grapes stuck on them. My legs shook and I felt suddenly weak as all the blood corpuscles in my body took a vote and made a unanimous decision to accumulate in one spot. 'Come on fellas,' I pleaded, 'leave some for the legs'. But it was no use and my entire being was concentrated into one little lump of turgid flesh. *Homo sapiens*? You must be joking. *Homo lunaticus erectus*.

'Er, good afternoon, madam,' I said weakly. 'I haven't come to buy a hat or anything, you see, what happened is this, I just leaned against that...'

'Save your breath, lover, you're going to need it,' she breathed huskily, sounding a bit like a man I once knew who smoked kippers in Fleetwood: he reckoned they were cheaper than a pipe. She moved towards me, her long lashes fluttering as she eyed my railwayman's trousers.

'Honey, I always said when it comes to the end of the world I want to go coming, if you know what I mean.' She slid her hand inside my shirt. 'You may only be a railwayman but I bet you like to go off the rails once in a while.' She pressed her open mouth on to mine and thrust her tongue in so far it took the fur off the back of my eyeballs.

Without ceremony she pushed me through a door I hadn't noticed before, at the back of the shop. It led into a lavishly decorated room, hung with bright crimson and orange silks, at the centre of which was a huge circular bed with pure silk sheets the colours of sunset. Hung round the walls were illustrations from all the world's great books on love: the *Karma Sutra, The Perfumed Garden, The Book of Salome, Scouting for Boys, Aero Modellers Monthly*. She undressed me hurriedly, her mouth moving over my body like a hot hoover. She flung off her own clothes. An odour of raw electric passion filled the air, like the ozone smell of colliding dodgem cars or the sorting shed at Whitby fish-dock.

'Take me,' she screamed, throwing herself backwards on the bed.

I took my glasses off and placed them gently on the dressing table. She became a pink blur with a bright red bushy triangle at the centre. I threw myself towards it. I missed. It hurt. An eleven-stone man landing on seven inches of engorged soft tissue doesn't make for true happiness.

I tried again, tears blinding my eyes. This time I impaled a pillow. 'Give me a clue,' I cried, staggering round the room, the pillow suspended from my jib. Her soft hands conducted me into the groves of

Venus and threw away the map, and for the next four hours, dear reader, as the folksongs say:

> ... we sported and played.
> I boarded her like a pirate cutter,
> Broadside to broadside at it we went
> Till me powder was gone and me bullets all spent.'

Then we had a cup of tea.
  At it again we went like two mad dogs.
  I nibbled her ears, she bit the inside of my thighs.
  I ran my tongue down her spine.
  She nibbled my shoulder.
  I pushed my tongue in her ears.
  She nibbled my bottom lip.
  I nibbled her top lip.
  Her teeth sank into my nose.
'I love a man with fire and passion in his bones,' she cried as I held a cold wet flannel to my bleeding nose and looked vaguely at her blurred face through eyes brimming with hot tears. Then, breathing like a steam roller going up a cobbled hill on a frosty morning, she threw me back on the bed and straddled me as though I was a 500 cc Kawasaki. She grabbed my ears and rode me up and down the bed like a Hell's Angel doing a ton across a ploughed field. I was almost unconscious with the pain from my twisted ears, my back had locked in spasm and the muscles in my legs were plaited with cramp. Just before I passed out she parked me up against a passing pillow and dismounted.

'Back in a tick,' she whispered, jumping from the bed. 'I'm just going for the handcuffs, sink plunger and cream caramel.' I grabbed my glasses as soon as she'd left the room, and searched for my clothes. All but the railwayman's boots had gone. I grabbed her gold sheath dress and, quickly donning it, hobbled

out in the boots towards the street. Before she could stop me I was out through the door and legging it off. I would rather be pecked to shreds than ridden to death on the Wall of Life, I thought.

The street was now strangely empty, save for the five thousand or so corpses strewn around. I looked skywards—there was no sign of the birds. Keeping to the deepening shadows I made my way in a gold sheath dress and railwayman's boots across London in the hurrying dusk like a metallic hunchback bent double with fear and post-coital fatigue.

There were bodies in every street I came to. As I passed Big Ben I looked up and saw that old, so well-known face smashed, the hands twisted, the great spring hanging down lifeless—it seemed a symbol of England's doom. An old man in uniform wobbled towards me.

'I tell yer, guv'nor, it's the bleedin' end. No wha' I mean? Them wossnames have done for old London tahn—' he gulped back his tears. 'Mean to say, guv'nor, just look rahnd yer, all them luverly buildings destroyed...'

'But the planners and developers knocked them down,' I said.

'Yers, mate, granted, but now them wossnames have gone even worse, inthey, narmean? They've done Big Ben in and' (he sobbed) 'the ravens have gorn from the Tahr ev Lunnen.'

'The ravens!'

'Yes mate, guv'nor, you know what they say: "When the ravens have gorn from the Tahr ev Lunnen, England's finished!" A gang of SAS-type wossnames flew down and beat the seed out of 'em. We're finished mate, narmean? Hitler couldn't do it, but them wossnames 'ave. The tube stations are full of people singin' "Run Rabbit Run" and "Hang out the Washin' on the Siegfried Line" but I tell you, mate, it's the end for London. We should have sold it to the Arabs when we had the chance.'

He turned and, before I could stop him, he'd walked into the Thames through the cold night air of Limehouse. His traffic warden's cap floating on the oily slick of the turning tide was the last I saw of him.

Fires were burning all over London, their smoke darkening the wintry sky, as I walked over Westminster Bridge. People were fleeing London in their thousands. Cars jammed bumper to bumper were streaming out, people with handcarts, bicycles, nuns on roller skates, milk floats full of Greek Cypriot waiters, a surging tide of humanity fleeing the Great Wen in best disaster novel prose. People were crying, wailing, tears streaming down their cheeks as they fled the smoking city in the face of the coming of the birds. A peeling poster on a hoarding read 'Life is better under the Con...' The rest was missing.

A group of drunks were breaking in the windows of a chemist's shop, looking for invalid wine and hangover cures. Signs of looting and the breakdown of civilization as we know it were everywhere. A city gent with a bowler hat and an umbrella was standing in the gutter shouting, 'I'm not going to pay my rates, I'm not going to pay my rates.'

'This is what would have happened if Benn had got in,' wheezed one middle-aged middle-class lady wheeling a handcart full of stuff she'd looted from Harrods, Selfridge's and Fortnum and Mason's. 'It's all the work of Moscow,' she wailed, disappearing into the night.

I walked through the darkening streets. The lights of old London were out—they must have got all the power supplies, too, I thought. It was strange to see London dark and silent. By Holborn and the Strand I made my way: where only the day before happy bustling crowds had thronged into the theatres, now there was only darkness and an oppressive stillness.

The hoardings proclaimed:
'*No Socks Please, We're Armenian*—now in its hundredth year.'

'*The Rat-trap*—will run forever.'

'*The Normans in Britain*—best bestiality in years'—*Evening Standard*.

'The tonic the West End has needed'—*Express*.

'The scenes of bestiality and cannibalism have the audience in the aisles'—*Guardian*.

I moved on, threading my way through the eye-dark streets. It was midnight by the time I got to Downing Street, having come via Islington as only somebody with no knowledge of London could have done. The Army was outside in its hundreds —tanks, armoured cars, weapons carriers— the street was dug up, trenches and sandbags were all round it and a caravan for the officers and Intelligence Corps was parked outside the door.

'I want to see the Prime Minister,' I said to a burly

Scotch Parachute Regiment Sergeant with teeth like a badly painted fence.

He eyed me up and down.

'Does yer mammy know you're oot, wee lassie?'

I hitched up the dress and flashed my credentials. 'MI5,' I said.

He undid his fly. 'M16,' he quipped, waving me through.

The PM was in the drawing-room with some important-looking military types. When I entered she dismissed them. 'Ah, Chuckles,' she said. 'Glad you made it.'

'Where's Flatfoot?'

'He's lying down in the basement with a bone,' she told me. 'Come, sit down.' She put her hand on my knee and poured me a large Scotch. 'Tomorrow we're going into an on-going war situation in the government bunker, but tonight you and I are going to get drunk, smashed as a wheelbarrow full of monkeys.'

When I woke up the next morning my head felt like ten pounds of half-boiled mince in a football casing. Something behind my eyes was trying to drill its way out and my tongue looked like a strip of astroturf. I rolled it round my mouth and it was like licking the inside of a jungle guerilla's boot after several thousand tadpoles had died in it. I'd had hangovers before, but this was the worst one I'd ever had. It felt as if I'd got up and put the wrong body on—I wasn't having a hangover, it was having me.

I looked at myself in the mirror. A pair of eyes gazed back from a stubbly grey face, like an old vest with a hedgehog inside, looking as though someone had thrown them on to it as an afterthought. The original blue of the pupils was now overpowered by the fiery tracery of surrounding red lines that had knitted together to weave a bright scarlet mat. My eyes resembled nothing so much as bluebottles on red flannel.

I croaked in what had once been a throat, and the PM swept into the bedroom. 'Hands off cocks, on socks,' she crowed. 'Out of the pit, rise and shine. We've got a busy day ahead of us.'

We sped up the M1 in the PM's bullet-proof Maestro, her hairdresser and speechwriter in the back with her husband, her bodyguard and Flatfoot.

'Not much traffic about,' I observed.

'In times of national emergency the motorways are sealed off to all but military traffic.'

'But what about the people trying to flee the cities?'

'Chuff 'em,' she said. 'We believe in people helping themselves, and taking more responsibilities on their own shoulders. They must do as they're told. People must stand on their own two feet and do exactly what we want them to do.' Her mouth closed firmly like a hen's ovipositor and her eyes stared ahead madly like valves on a pressure cooker. In other circumstances, I decided, she would have been on her own in a room with rubber walls, wearing an overcoat back to front.

'Where are we going?' I asked.

'To the nearest government bunker in the Cotswolds.'

'Bourton-on-the-Water?'

'I don't mind if I do,' her husband muttered, coming round again, a copy of *The Boys' Own Book of Torture* under his arm. She hit him with her handbag, and he sank back in the seat.

An hour later, we swung off the motorway in to typically English leafy country roads that got narrower and narrower the further we went until eventually the car swung through the gates of what seemed to be a nursing home. Old people bent over walking-sticks dotted the lawn. The ivy-covered front of a Georgian mansion stood before us at the end of a long tree-lined path.

'Is this it?' I asked. But before I got an answer the ivy-covered front split down the middle, the old people folded flat and we found ourselves speeding down a brightly-lit subterranean tunnel into the heart of a great hill. They had all been cardboard cut-outs. Men in blue overalls were busy everywhere. A sign on the wall said: 'Welcome to Bunkersville UK, twinned with Krakatoa.' At the heart of the network of tunnels was the Nerve Centre, UK. We got out of the car.

'Are we here, my dear? Where's the bar?' The Prime Minister's husband asked. She floored him with another blow from her handbag. He lay there like the aftermath of an explosion in an Oxfam shop. 'Pick him up,' she said to her hairdresser. 'Give him some slippery elm and put him to bed.'

We walked the corridors until we came to the Central Communications Rooms. There, hundreds of the military were bent over row after row of glowing screens; an illuminated wall had a schematic chart of the British Isles and Western Europe with digital read-outs, trajectory lines and glowing lights. I was conscious of being at the nerve centre of a mighty universe. Outside that bunker England trembled and feared, believing that those in power had the situation in their grasp, not knowing that those in power had in fact no idea at all but were acting on the principle, 'When in doubt make decisions—any sort of decision—it gives the people confidence in you,' a principle by which all governments have fooled people ever since the first caveman decided to make himself chief. As we walked in everyone looked up. The PM nodded at the men around her. She smiled, showing her teeth, and four of the men fainted.

'Gentlemen,' she said, indicating myself, 'this is Mr Chuckles. Don't worry about the dress, it's just a front. He has information that may be valuable to us. He was personally present at the very first outbreak of ornithological counterpersonnel engagements.'

'What does that mean?' I asked.

'You were there when the little fiend ripped Rudolpho's head off, you weary Willie,' she muttered from the side of her mouth.

I realized then that nobody had given a thought to Rudolpho for days. It seemed a lifetime since he had died. Then again, if I'd been a butterfly or an amoeba it *would* have been a lifetime ago. I would have been born, married, had forty thousand children and died.

'Now, Tredwell,' she cracked, 'what's the latest news?'

A stringy individual with thinning hair combed forward from the back of his head like a badly-fitting beret stepped forward in a cloud of dandruff. When he spoke, he sounded like a frog with a man in its throat. 'Well, as you probably know, Prime Minister, the whole of London is in a state of utter chaos. The few people who are left there are camped out in the parks. The Army is managing to shift the bodies, but key communication centres are inoperable and a lot of buildings have been destroyed.'

'Which ones?' she asked.

'Well, mainly those built since 1960: Centre Point, the Post Office Tower, the Knightsbridge Barracks, the South Bank, and the Barbican.'

I couldn't believe it. Budgies with architectural taste!

'They've also destroyed every hamburger bar, every souvenir and jeans shop in Oxford Street, and the birdcage in Regent's Park Zoo.'

Incredible! They did have taste!

'Towards four am this morning they vanished northwards. All the tracking stations in Britain have been destroyed and the satellite stations' receiving dishes are out of action.'

'So how are you tracking them?' she asked.

'Well, em, boy scouts with semaphore flags are standing on every hill. As soon as they see the budgies pass, they flag the message on down the line to us here.'

The Prime Minister spat a plug of tobacco into a waste-paper bin.

'Thank God for Baden-Powell,' she muttered, then her face darkened. 'Fudge,' she cursed, 'I knew it was the Russians. Now they've knocked out all our early warning systems they can just step in and take us over. Somebody's made a right horlicks of this.'

'I don't think that's quite true, PM. Just before our screens went blank at three am we traced a similar-sized cloud of budgies heading towards Moscow.'

She gasped. 'World domination,' she whispered almost beneath her breath, 'but that was my idea.' She flung herself into a chair before the command console. 'Get me the White House,' she snapped. 'Can we still do that?'

'Yes. All lines are functional, but only just.'

The screen before her glowed dully as an operative punched a code into a keyboard matrix. There was a pause of a few seconds then the face of the President of the United States appeared on the screen. He was picking his nose with the single-minded attention of a thrush trying to get a snail out of its shell. He pulled something out and stared at it attentively for a few seconds before wiping it off on the side of his desk. He noticed the lit screen on front of him and half-turning to somebody out of vision in the room said,

'Okay, Harvey, switch it on and I'll talk to the stupid Limey bitch.'

He turned to face the screen. We appeared before him, glowing. 'Oh, hello, Prime Minister, how are things at your end? We seem to have a little trouble getting through to our Embassy in London, some kind of electric storm or something, all the lines are down. I bet my bottom dollar it's the work of those no-good pagan anti-Christ heart of darkness commie mothers. The sooner we get into a position where we can wipe them off the face of the earth with pre-emptive nuke strikes the better.'

The PM cut in. 'Mr President, the lines between your Embassy in London and the White House have gone down because London itself has been virtually destroyed by a flock of killer budgies.'

The President blinked and in his best John Wayne style said, 'Like Hell they have.' He thought for a minute. 'Have you nuked Moscow yet?'

'We're not sure that they're from Moscow.'

'They must've come from Moscow, these budgets or whatever they're called. Only the commies would do a thing like that. What are they, anyway?'

'What?'

'Budgets?'

'They're budgies, and they're a sort of bird.'

'Like Hell they are.' He fell asleep for a brief second before jerking awake again. 'Look, you want Tocas J. Wamburger the Fourth Junior out there with you. He's our senior tactician Western Europe. We've probably got some chemicals or germs or something we can spray on them. Tocas, he's your man. He'll probably want to nuke Moscow just in case, anyway, so tell him from me if it's A-okay with God, it's A-okay with me.'

Just then somebody passed him a piece of paper. He looked at it blankly for a while, then realized it was a script. A large piece of ceiling plaster fell on his head. Covered in plaster dust and grinning inanely, a thin trickle of blood running down his forehead, he started reading monotonously from the paper, hardly looking up, his eyes glancing feverishly at the symbols trying to translate them into words.

'Em, well Prime Minister, it's been absolutely marvellous. Talking to you I really admire the way. You British have maintained as an island race the sense. Of destiny that has been thrust upon you in the tide and course of...'

A flurry of bird's wings filled the air and the screen went blank.

The Prime Minister paled a little then seemed to steel herself with resolve. 'Is Wamburger here yet?'

An assistant nodded.

'Bring him to me.'

The assistant trotted off, and an RAF technician watching one of the screens at the bottom of the room called to her, 'Prime Minister, the Third West Riding Rover Scout Troop report that the birds seemed to have settled and landed.'

'Whereabouts?'

'Somewhere in the North they lost contact with them. In the Leeds-Bradford area it was. They were heading north-west.'

'Of course!' It came to me in a flash. 'Ilkley Moor,'.I blurted out.

'What are you talking about?' she asked. Flatfoot barked enthusiastically and pawed at my leg.

'"Then worms will come and eat thee up. Eat thee up, on Ilkley Moor baht 'at.". It's the old song. It's the clue on the dressing-room ceiling!!!'

Tocas J. Wamburger the Fourth Junior stood in the doorway, a short-cropped grizzled head on top of a mountain of medals. He had so much metal work jangling about his corpulent frame that every magnetic instrument in the room went into spasm. He waddled to a halt, a scrap merchant's dream, and saluted with a podgy pink hand that looked like a scale model of a sea anemone.

'Tocas J. Wamburger the Fourth Junior, ma'am, US Armed Forces Europe, supreme Allied commander, NATO defence staff supremo Western Hemisphere, pastor of the Church of God and Spiritual Snake Handlers Alberquerque and an all-fire all-round commie-hating, shit-kicking son of a gun.'

He took a folding guitar out of his pocket and launched into song, hitting ear-jarring notes and singing through his nose in a tuneless shriek, punctuated by 'yip's and 'hell yeah's that sounded like someone beating a chicken to death with a dinner gong.

> Ever since I set my eyes
> On my mama's apple pie
> I knew what it meant to be free
> From the Statue of Liberty's torch
> To the swing seat on the porch
> There are some things America means to me.
> Soda fountains after school
> Catching catfish in the pool
> Weenee bakes, Trick or Treat and Halloween
> Disney Land, the CIA, General Motors and My Lai
> These are things America means to me.

He sang the first two verses and played a quick instrumental on the guitar, grinning round him like a geriatric Johnny Cash. Clearing his throat and spitting into the corner he started on the next verses.

> 'Just forget the Ku Klux Klan
> Three Mile Island, Vietnam,
> Hiroshima, agent orange and the rest
> For Norman Rockwell's prints
> Are my American chintz
> Of all things American, he's the best.
> Pecan pie and malted milk, oh
> Nagasaki and Sergeant Bilko,
> Bambi, the Mafia and the Seven Dwarfs
> Senator McCarthy and Oak Ridge
> And the Chappaquidick Bridge...

He rallentandoed and in a reprise of the tune of the last two lines sang, in a voice that was getting husky, 'I must declare my everlasting love of America, and my hatred of commies, hippies, faggots, Catholics, Jews, intellectuals, but most of all—Ruskies. This is what America means to me.'

When he finished there was a burst of applause from the Prime Minister.

'Bravo, General, those are the words that echo my sentiments exactly. We must fight them on the beaches, we must fight them in the streets and we must what-d'you-ma-call 'em . . . be prepared to kick them in the cheeky bits if we are to preserve our way of life. But I am afraid to say, it rather looks as though your President is having his share of troubles too. We've totally lost contact with Washington in the last hour, and all our attempts to regain contact with them have failed. However, we do seem to have some good news, we seem to have located the headquarters—or at least the temporary resting place—of these fiendish and inhuman creatures. They're in a place in the North called Ilkley Moor, which my experts tell me is a bare and windswept heath on the edges of Leeds and Bradford, which again my experts tell me are themselves on the edge of civilization. Now, you Americans are experts on mass destruction in the name of freedom. Have you any ideas on how we can deal with the threat?'

Tocas J. Wamburger the Fourth Junior scratched his crotch and shifted his bubble gum from one side of his flabby WASP jaw to the other. His jowls flapped like damp washing in a high wind, and the bags beneath his eyes hung like pelicans' crops. He scratched his grizzled head. Remotely, from the dim recesses of his brain, an idea crawled forward sluggishly on all fours, like a drunk climbing a butter mountain. Then gleefully he spelt it out.

'Zap the bastards.'

'What?' the PM muttered.

'Nuke the commie crows.'

'But the fall-out—Leeds, Bradford.'

'Leeds, Shmeeds. You can't make an omlette without a few civilian lateral pre-emptive negations.'

'You mean deaths,' I said.

'Sure—mega-deaths, or as we in the military would nomenclate it, the interpolation or extra-polation of large-scale secessions of viable parameters among the civilian population.'

'You're a pillock,' I muttered.

'Correct, sonny, but so long as the rest of the world never finds out, I'm also a very powerful pillock. These Russian birds have got to be zeroed, negated, nuked, negatived survival-wise.'

The Prime Minister stepped forward, placatingly. 'Now look, General Wamburger.' She switched on her reasonable voice. 'I can see that your ideas have a certain directness about them that appeals to me. After all, we do have these nuclear weapons hanging round and nothing to do with them and it seems a shame not to use them, I agree. Particularly since the taxpayer has paid for them already, and you know a lot of those taxpayers are old people—the sick and the young who've suffered so much for so long. But there are rather a lot of people living in the Leeds, Bradford and Halifax area, and you know some of them are very old. And you know some of them in fact do vote Conservative, and if one wipes them out before a General Election, one could find one's popularity going down. You know, it would be hard for one to convince people that we were a caring and considerate party. Although it is the North of England we are talking about and it doesn't really matter all that much, I still feel that before we go for the more extreme methods of getting rid of those birds we must try something a little less catastrophic. And you know—'

He cut her short. 'Well, you may be right, your majesty, but I still think we should zap the bastards.'

I stepped forward. 'Ahem, Prime Minister.' For the first time Tocas J. Wamburger the Fourth Junior looked at me properly.

'He's a goddam fruit,' he muttered to himself.

I'd forgotten that I was still wearing my gold lamé dress and railwayman's boots. The Prime Minister turned round. 'What?'

'It seems to me that if the budgies have gone to ground on Ilkley Moor, then we ought to go up there.'

'It could be dangerous,' she said. 'I mean one could get hurt, couldn't one?'

'True,' I said. 'But it's the only way of finding out exactly what's going on.'

'I know exactly what's going on,' she said. 'People are dying; dying spelt aarg, mng, aarg.'

'I agree, Prime Minister,' Wamburger said, scratching his crotch again. 'I think we should stay here safe and nuke the bastards.'

The Prime Minister moved to one of the screens. 'Get me General Sir Harry Bollo, KC,' she said.

Bollo's face appeared on the screen. 'Er, yes, PM, you've heard the news?'

'Yes,' she snapped back. 'I want you to get your men on to Ilkley Moor at once. Surround the entire Moor, locate the hiding-place of these feathered fiends and deploy the SAS, the Marines, the SBS, the Gurkhas and the Band of the Sutherland and Argyll Highlanders.'

I interrupted them. 'Prime Minister,' I said, 'there is just one possible place they could be holed up.'

'Where's that?' she asked.

'I remember reading as a boy, in the comics,' I said,

'that there's a cave on Ilkley Moor where Wilson the famous athlete used to live and train. It's big enough inside for a couple of million budgies. That could be the place you're looking for.'

She turned to the face on the screen. 'Did you hear that, Bollo?'

'Yes, your majes—I mean, ma'am,' he answered.

She said, 'Fine, carry on, you know your orders.'

Bollo saluted on the screen. 'Certainly your—I mean, ma'am, I'll get on with it straight away. I'm on my way up there right now.'

The screen faded.

At that moment a cough behind us announced the arrival of Rear Admiral Rodney Entry, RN, Commander of the Fleet. 'The Navy is at your service and waiting,' he said, coming to a halt and saluting.

The Prime Minister looked at him. 'You're wasting your time. There's nothing you can do, Rodney.'

'Why not?' he asked, his lower lip trembling.

'Because Ilkley Moor is not on the sea coast.'

'Are you sure? Is it English?'

'Well, it's north of Watford.'

'In that case, it probably isn't.'

'It's in Yorkshire,' I said.

The Navy chap blenched visibly.

'Yorkshire? I've heard of that before. Aren't there a lot of socialists up there?'

At the word socialist, the Prime Minister fainted outright. Her scriptwriter knelt over her.

He looked up. 'She often reacts like that when you mention that word suddenly.' He took a flask out of his pocket and pressed it to the PM's lips. She took a sip, then a gulp, then several mouthfuls. Slowly she revived, and in a few seconds was back on her feet. I took a sniff of the flask. It was a mixture of diluted sulphuric acid and ammonia.

'That's better,' she said, adjusting her skirt and

patting her hair back into place. 'Now where was I? Ah yes, Rodney, there's absobalolutely nothing you can do.'

'Well that's a dashed shame PM. A lot of my chaps are keen to have a go—senior service and all that sort of thing. We were sort of rather sort of hoping, don't you know, for a bit of the action.'

'Bloody lion's share don't you mean,' somebody at the back muttered.

'Now Rodders, there's a good chap, take a couple of your gunboats, and go and bombard somewhere no one will miss—Glasgow or somewhere like that.'

Rodney seemed pleased.

The Prime Minister watched him go, then slapped Wamburger heartily on the back. 'Come, General!' she shouted. 'We have work to do in the North!'

In her special car we sped northwards up the M6. The General eyed my dress suspiciously. I winked at him and patted him on the knee, then I leaned forward and tapped the Prime Minister on the shoulder. 'Prime Minister,' I said, 'I've had an idea. We're going to be passing fairly close to Manchester, aren't we?'

'Mmm,' she nodded. 'Well, what's that got to do with anything?'

'I think it's going to be worth our while to seek out the advice of a learned sage that I happen to know lives near there. I've never met him but I've heard that he's a genius. We're passing not far away, and anything's worth a try in these trying times. He's said to have the wisdom of Solomon, the mystic knowledge of Nostradamus, and the footwork of Georgie Best.'

'Who are you talking about?'

'They call him the Magus, the Guru of Salford.'

THIS CUSHION IS NOT RESPONSIBLE FOR THE NOISES YOU ARE ABOUT TO HEAR!

Two hours later we were pulling off the motorway and driving down through Salford. Around us was a forest of high-rise blocks of council flats, everywhere deserted and abandoned. Scraps of paper and filth blew along the streets, dead dogs and cats rotted in the gutters, rubble filled the spaces between the towers. The grey concrete walls of the houses were sprayed with graffiti and we drove through underpasses covered in obscene aerosol slogans. Some of them caught my eye.

DON'T VOTE, IT ONLY ENCOURAGES THEM.
GOD IS ALIVE AND WELL, AND WORKING IN A CHIPPY IN WIGAN.
IF THIS IS A GOVERNMENT, I'M A FISH.

Everywhere there was an air of destruction, dereliction, desolation and despair.

'My God,' said the Prime Minister, thumping her knee with her clenched fist, 'to think that those birds could have done all this.'

'The birds didn't do all this,' I said. 'The planners and developers did it.'

We swung into a crescent called Shangri La Close and made our way to the top floor of an abandoned high-rise block. By the time we got to the sixteenth floor the Prime Minister and I were choking and sobbing for breath and Flatfoot's tongue was hanging out. Wamburger and the Prime Minister's husband sat in the car, drinking and reading *The Encyclopedia of Murder and Mayhem*. We kicked open the door of the only flat that still had its windows in. The guru sat cross-legged on a cushion, reading *Health and Efficiency*.

He was a thin ascetic man with the hollow burning eyes that proclaimed him either a mystic or a Vimto addict or a haemorrhoids sufferer. About his head was a turban, and his only other article of clothing was a Mickey Mouse watch. The Prime Minister stiffened visibly when she saw that he was naked. He seemed unconcerned by her concern. Without looking up he murmured 'Welcome,' in a voice as soft as a good malt whisky being poured on velvet. 'I was expecting you,' he said.

I prostrated myself before him. The Prime Minister followed suit. There then followed one of the strangest conversations it's been my misfortune to be party to. I don't know whether it was because of his strict vegetarian diet, his fasting or for some

64

other reason entirely, but every so often, as he spoke, the Magus broke wind loudly. His mystical statements were punctuated by a series of thunderous farts of various length and resonance, of which he himself seemed unconscious, but which threatened to render us unconscious as well. After a while it seemed almost as though he used them as punctuation in place of commas, colons, semi-colons, full stops and speech marks.

'We seek knowledge and wisdom, O Magus of Salford,' I said.

He answered in a sing-song voice, 'When the heaviness of the stars' (*prrrp*) 'weighs upon your breast' (*paroop*) 'how can a pin-prick of light hurt any more?' (*Whummmmf*.) 'A small mouse' (*brump*) 'can nibble away the foundations of a palace.' (*Whaaarp*.) 'Today' (*prroop*) 'is the last day of your' (*boorf*) 'past.' (*Wrwp*.)

'I'm staggered by your wisdom,' observed the Prime Minister, her eyes watering and the muscles round her neck twitching madly.

'Oh those (*pooop*),' said the Magus (*brumfff*), 'I got them out of a Christmas cracker.' (*Paaarrp*.) 'Now, what can I do for you?' (*Booomf*.)

'We want to know how to defeat the budgies,' she said.

(*Pooomf*) 'Buy gold,' instructed the Magus. (*Warp*) 'The tree that bends with the wind,' he raised himself up on one cheek and let one go that said *Whamfffprap*, 'its plums fall off.'

'Is that all you have to say?' the Prime Minister asked, visibly gagging.

'If you can't buy gold' (*prp*) 'buy land' (*poop*), 'it's sure to come back in a couple of years' time.'

'But have you nothing else to say?'

'Yes,' said the Magus, 'unlucky for some' (*poop*) 'number 9.'

'Is that all?' demanded the Prime Minister.

'Look, hatchet face,' said the Magus, 'you haven't even offered me any money yet.'

'How much do you want?' asked the Prime Minister.

'Well, a couple of hundred quid would tide me over for a rainy day.'

The Prime Minister reached in her handbag, pulled out a handful of hundred-pound notes and threw them towards him. 'Now,' she said, 'what can you tell us?'

'Well,' replied the Magus, 'as a parting shot I'll leave you with this.' He raised himself up on one cheek and dropped one that started off as a mosquito-like whine and ended up like the roar of an angry baboon: *Wzeezeegaarodgrodgrodgfums-waarp*. 'Screw the poor.'

'But we're doing that already,' the Prime Minister protested.

'End of consultation,' said the Magus and, picking up his book, began reading again.

We bowed our way out backwards, I with my hanky to my eyes, and the Prime Minister with her head in her handbag.

'And shut the bloody door (*paarp*),' said the Magus.

Half an hour after climbing the Guru's stairs we were on our way down the motorway again.

'He seemed as nutty as a fruit cake,' she muttered. 'How did he end up like that?'

'Total isolation, long periods of starvation, exposure to intense cold.'

'He trained himself through yoga, self-denial, fasting? Excellent.'

'No, he was an old age pensioner.'

We pulled off the road and drove on through the outskirts of Ilkley. The once-thriving middle-class

Yorkshire town was empty. The bijou villas built on the woolly backs of Yorkshire sheep and the bare backs of Yorkshire people were deserted-some of them showed all the signs of having recently been looted, for garden gnomes lay smashed in tasteful acts of iconoclasm, plastic alpine pools lay empty, the windmills at their side still and unturning, with the little milkmaids and winding men hanging slackly in the breeze. We turned away from the town and headed up towards the moor. Flatfoot started jumping up and down on the seat and barking at the sheep as we passed them. I grabbed his collar and pulled him back down again. He still growled. I tapped his nose sharply with a newspaper and he was quiet.

'What in tarnation's gotten into him?' asked Wamburger, scratching his crotch.

'He thinks he's a dog,' I said. 'He ate a tin of dog food a few days back and now he thinks he's a dog.'

'Goddam crazy mother. A fruit in a gold dress with a G-man who thinks he's a dog. You English are crazy.' He looked ahead for a moment, then a thought crossed his mind like a lone duck on Lake Windermere on a misty day. 'What sort of a dog does he think he is?'

'Police dog.'

'Holy poop. You limeys are plumb loco.'

Dusk was falling and crows were calling in the bare black winter trees when we left the last streets of the town behind and climbed up on to the moor edge. Ahead of us, a glow on the sky showed where the military were encamped, and as the car crested a small rise we saw before us the arc lights of a hurriedly-erected compound. Strung out in a two-mile-long semicircle facing the rocky cliffs were the guns and armour, rocket launchers and men of one of the finest armies in the world. Facing them across half a mile of heathery moor were twenty million budgies. It seemed an uneven match. Even now, all these years later, it still does. Yet how were we to know in that fateful time the secret diabolic powers those budgies had? We jerked to a halt before some SAS men whose faces looked as though they had been put together in concrete and scars from an identikit. They peered into the car, saw the Prime Minister, and waved us through.

In the centre of the compound, in a large control centre made from four caravans joined together, General Sir Harry Bollo, KC was studying a map. Previously I had only seen him on the video screen at Bunkersville UK, now I had the chance to study him in the flesh.

He was a tall stringy man with hands that seemed to be composed entirely of knuckles. Somebody had stolen his chin and had instead blessed him with ears that, with his military short haircut, made him look like a male model for turnstiles. When he smiled, as he did frequently, his teeth—his very English teeth—stood neatly to attention in his mouth. His face was above all a British face, a face that had cowed native peoples the Empire over, from Aden to Bombay, Galway to Nairobi, a face bronzed by the radiant sun of an Empire that has tinted six tenths of the map pink, a face washed by English rain, kissed by an English breeze, a face that could send men unquestioning to their deaths, the face in short of a right dozy pillock. He stepped towards us, all ears and green fatigues—like a gherkin with tail fins. He shook hands with the Prime Minister and Wamburger. He was just about to shake hands with Flatfoot when Flatfoot started growling and snapped at him. I put him outside, he cocked his leg up against the Land Rover then went to sleep.

'So what's the plan?' the Prime Minister asked.

'Well, ma'm, there doesn't seem to be too much activity at the moment, don't you know. We've got the enemy surrounded, our chaps have dug in and have established forward defence positions and observation posts, etc, etc. The birds are holed up in a huge cave three quarters of a mile northward,' he pointed. 'But as far as we can see nothing's moved for simply ages. They seem to have gone to ground, regrouping as it were, don't you know, etc, etc. We sent some of the SAS men out a couple of hours ago to do a recce.'

'What happened?' she asked anxiously.

'Well, to be honest, ma'm, it was a bit of a deuced wash-out, don't you know. Some budgies flew over just before you arrived and dropped—er—four pair of ears on us.'

'The diabolical fiends,' she muttered.

'Yes, quite. Well, we've just had a signal from the USAF satellite. Apparently the White House has been totally destroyed and the President has had to flee for his life. Their message was garbled, but it looks as though they're having the same problems that we are. Their, em, birds seem to have holed up in the Grand Canyon.'

'The only answer is to nuke the bastards,' said Wamburger, beating his chest like Tarzan. 'Aaaagh! Nuke Moscow, nuke Leningrad, nuke—erm, nuke—erm . . . Where the hell else is there in Russia? Nuke everywhere.'

'Ah well, that's just it,' said General Sir Harry Bollo, KC. 'It looks as if Ivan is having exactly the same problem that we are. Apparently the Politburo chiefs have had to skeddadle from the Kremlin and the budgies, after destroying most of the major cities, are encamped somewhere in the Urals.'

'World domination,' the PM whispered to herself. 'It really isn't fair, I did think of it first.'

Bollo, KC spoke again. 'With your permission, PM, we would like to have a couple of shots at them with some of the heavy stuff, don't you know.'

'Jolly good idea, what were you thinking of?'

'Well we—, I mean, that is, Jemmers and I' (he indicated another chinless Hooray-Henry who even in full combat gear with his face blacked up still looked like an interior designer or a Harrods floor-walker) 'we thought we'd lob a few heavy cans over first, just to test the enemy's metal. After what they did to the RAF and some of our chaps in London, the mob feel they'd like the chance to draw a bit of blood, don't you know, whip up there, have a couple of potshots and do a quick bunk.'

'Carry on, jolly good.' She slapped her thigh in jubilation.

Bollo, KC turned to Jemmers. 'Jemmers, er, send Bilbo in with six forty-sevens, tell them to get within a few hundred yards and await orders.'

We watched the scene through observation slits as six armoured rocket launchers rumbled across the moor towards the crags. Above, a lark sang in the watery sunlight as though all this madness was a million miles away and England was at peace again. England as it once was—the cities gently crumbling into ruins, the island race learning once again the joys of tribal warfare and cannibalism, and the money fleeing into Swiss bank vaults faster than swallows departing at a summer's end.

The HF receiver cracked. The operator turned, looking anxiously at Bollo, and tuned it more finely. 'Apple Tango Three to Noddy, Apple Tango Three to Noddy. Do you read me?'

The operator spoke. 'I read you Apple Tango Three, positions established, sir.'

'Roger, Apple Tango Three, proceed firing at will, four rounds rapid per carrier then hold fire.'

Through a slit between the sandbags we watched the launchers recoil as smoke engulfed them, and a fraction of a second later the roar of the launchings reached our ears as four times six rockets were unleashed with their deadly cargoes towards the cliffs. What happened next appeared blurred and indistinct, but we suddenly saw the missiles swerve away from their target, and then turn completely round until they headed back towards their launchers. In the misty confusion of the moment I saw men leap from the carriers and run wildly in all directions just before the missiles struck and blasted six good-sized craters in the peat and broom, and a lot of expensive men and equipment were spread across the wide Yorkshire skies.

'Good Lord,' muttered the PM. 'What do I do now?'

The Prime Minister's speechwriter blenched. 'I'll nip round the back and write some copy, PM,' he whispered unctuously.

She butted him between the eyes. 'You stupid weary Walter,' she snarled. 'I want to destroy them, not get them to vote for me.'

He curled up in a foetal position in a corner and gnawed his knuckles, whimpering.

'No survivors, sir,' the radio operator offered.

'Tough titty,' said Bollo. 'Some of my best men there. Fish and chip mob generally, but some solid types, don't you know.'

Wamburger spluttered with rage. 'Those goddam commie crows must have a secret weapon. They just turned those mothers round.'

'We've got a video of the strike from our forward cameras,' offered the tech op. A screen lit up and we watched the events of the previous seven minutes re-form before our eyes. 'This is the ultimate,' I thought, 'action replay on World War Three. Watch yourself dying in Sony vision.'

'Slow down the action, Jenkins, old man,' the co droned. We watched the carriers lumbering across rough moorland and tussocky grass that only a few days before had been tramped over by earnest bearded hikers with rucksacks on their way for a pint at Dick Hudson's pub, sweet English earth that as the evening sun fell in the west would have resonated to the rhythmic thumping of lovers' bottoms, knees and thighs, celebrating a ritual as old as life itself: the mass Yorkshire Sunday Evening Nooky Festival. The cameras paused, a digital read-out at the side of the video screen sped up as the operator wound the tape on. We watched the launching of the missiles, and he slowed the recording down again so that we could see the individual missiles travelling in a staggered pack towards the millstone grit. A coloured flurry appeared at the top left-hand corner of the frame.

'Freeze frame,' barked Bollo, KC. The picture locked and the operator punched the switch that magnified the portion of the screen in question. It was unbelievable. Twenty-four budgies in a V-type formation were leaving the rocky cave, flying towards the missiles. At a command, the operator moved the tape forward frame by frame and we watched in silence as the budgies broke formation, intercepted the missiles and, straddling them like cowboys, used their own wings to turn them about and direct them towards the carriers, leaping aside and flying away only at the last moment, the last budgie giving an unmistakable V sign in the direction of the camera. Wamburger was the first to speak.

'Holy poop! This time the cack really has hit the fan. Those birds are out of sight!!'

'Yes, rather a tricky one this, don't you know,' said Bollo, KC. 'They've been doing the same thing with tear gas and rubber bullets.'

'Did you notice something else?' I asked.

'What?' asked the PM.

'Look at the budgies again, astride those rockets.'

The operator spooled back, and froze the frame in a one-shot of a single budgie astride a missile.

'What are the dimensions of those missiles?' I asked Bollo, KC.

'What, Cutlass? Let me see: length with booster, 3·7 m; length of missile, 2·3 m, diameter of missile, 0·37 m. Why do you ... Good God, I see what you mean! Those budgies must be over three foot tall!'

We spent an uneasy night, sleeping in turns (although beds would have been better) watching the screen for any sign of activity and drinking countless cups of coffee laced with dark rum. Wamburger got so drunk on coffee he tried to put his hand up the Prime Minister's skirt. She floored him with a savage karate chop that would have killed him had not his cerebral cortex been protected by several rolls of flesh and the sash of the Grand Order of Chipmunks.

'Did you learn that from the SAS?' I asked.

'No, Harrods in the January sales.'

Gradually throughout the night news came in from what was left of the world's communication systems. It didn't present a pretty picture. In four days, civilization as we knew it had been destroyed—perhaps completely. Cities had been deserted by their inhabitants, leaving them to the corpses and the carrion crows; disease was beginning to be a major problem; thousands were dying of simple ailments like dandruff and veruccas; millions were roaming the countryside, starving and lawless; the very fabric of society had crumbled. In our own Britain, jewel in a silvery sea, the BBC had been silenced. *The Times* was unpublished, the churches empty, bingo halls closed. The Empire on which the sun was never going to set was now very much in the dark. Everywhere else the same story came in: from Australia to Iceland, from Andora to Tierra del Fuego, the domestic *parakeetus parakeeti* had arisen, decimated the population, and destroyed life as it had been known. All attempts to stop the birds had failed—bombs had been carried back and dropped on the bombers, bullets and rockets turned aside, aircraft brought down, tanks destroyed and individual soldiers pecked to pieces. A group of Australian soldiers sent on a mission against the budgies that were hiding around Ayers Rock came back seemingly intact, but babbling. It was only discovered after a medical examination that they had all been given complete frontal lobotomies. The dawn came pitifully slowly, and a group of high-ranking military officials arrived one by one throughout the night.

They huddled in groups, looked at maps and talked in numbers and capital letters. 'Well, I think the RHA and the LRA TGW should take some FV4030's and a couple of FV102's and try and take them from the left and right, while the Gurkhas and the Jocks take the middle.' Another coughed before saying: 'Well, what about the SAS abseiling down from the top, lobbing in a few cans of quiet juice and taking them out with a few rounds rapid?'

'There are approximately twenty million budgies in those caves,' said another. 'I think the only way you'll wipe them out is germ warfare.'

'How are you going to introduce the germs to the budgies?' I asked from the dark corner where I'd slumped in a camp chair. 'Are you going to send a painted hen in with measles, or a rubber budgie with fowlpest or Parkinson's disease?'

'Who is this woman?' asked an elderly officer with a face like a bucket of spam and a moustache that looked as though two grey squirrels had tried to use his nostrils as boltholes and had got stuck with their tails hanging out.

'The name's Chuckles,' I said. 'I was in at this show right from the start, I'm working with the PM.' He backed off a bit at that, though he still eyed me suspiciously from time to time and I heard him mutter 'Bertie Wooftah' under his breath occasionally.

The PM yawned and stretched, standing up from her chair. The military, noting her, stood to attention, saluting wildly like tic-tac men with St. Vitus Dance.

'Has anybody here seen my husband?' she asked.

'Yes, PM, he's in the mess tent at the moment having a few stiffeners as he calls them. He says the damp on these moors has got through to his bones and he needed something to warm him up. He's had enough to burn a town down already. There's a policeman with a chain round his neck, walking about on all fours, with him.'

'Fudge!' she said. 'I shall smack him when I see

him. Now, gentlemen, to business. No weary Willies here.' The night's reports were given to her. While she read them, Wamburger came slowly to his senses and crawled off to be noisily sick in a clump of heather and broom. 'Warck, warck, gerdaw, gerdaw,' he cried. From across the heath crows and ducks answered him back. 'Warck, warck, gerdaw, gerdaw,' came back the answers from some very confused ducks, who were finding themselves the victims of what would, in human terms, have been an obscene phone call. The PM strode to the middle of the room.

'Gentlemen. The situation stands like this. Every country of any standard of civilization in the world has been reduced to ruins by these birds—America, Russia, France, Australia, Italy, Spain, Greece, the entire continent of Europe almost—and we don't know yet why they've done it. I suspect that the birds are after world domination.' There were gasps of astonishment. 'Tredlow, I want you to send a signal to the Americans and the Russians inviting what's left of their governments to meet here with a view to having a summit meeting and seeing if together we can thrash out the problem. Gentlemen,' she pointed to me, 'this is Mr Eric Chuckles. He was in at this show from the top, and has quite a bit of useful information concerning the birds. However, I think we should wait and see what the Russian and American answers are before we make any more moves. Our policy in the meantime shall be one of containment.'

Some coffee was brought in by a young WRAC corporal who eyed me in my dress in a quizzical way and smiled and winked at me.

'Prime Minister,' I asked, 'is there any possibility that I could get a change of clothes, I feel a bit stupid dressed like this.'

'Surely,' she replied. 'Em, Bollo do you have any

kit you could sort him out with?'

'Certainly,' replied Bollo. 'Corporal, take Mr Chuckles to the Quartermaster's Store and have him kitted out with some combat gear right away.'

I followed the corporal out. Her hips swung in a non-militaristic manner and I was ashamed to find myself have non-militaristic thoughts about her as I followed. She didn't speak as the QM piled my kit up high: shirts, khaki trousers, boots, the lot were dumped on my outstretched arms. Outside the stores she stared at me brazenly and nodded up the hill.

'You can change in my caravan if you like,' she said sultrily, her eyes going over me like a burglar's hands in a drawerful of loot, leaving no mistake in my mind at all as to what her inner meanings were.

The front half of the caravan was equipped as an office—it was obviously the place at which she did her military work—while in the back was a neat little bedroom with a large bed, curtains, and all the possible comforts that a military caravan could provide. Obviously the place where she did her off-limits work. It looked down on to the compound and across the moor. We went into the bedroom. She locked the door behind us, breathing heavily she advanced towards me in F formation. She slid her hand up my dress and stroked my thighs. She fastened her lips on mine, wet and hot, her mouth covered my mouth, her tongue parted my lips and flickered in and out like a moth round a candle. Her lips pressed on my lips, her thighs pressed against my thighs, her belly ground into my belly, her boot pressed against my throat.

Her boot! It was my boot. I put the clothes down and grabbed her again. I undid the blouse; WD issue, khaki, one. My hands slipped it off. I caressed the cups, double D, on the brassière, khaki, nylon, one, and undid the catch of the same, releasing two globes of firm hot flesh to swing free to my touch. I slid off skirt, dark green, one, tights, brown, pairs one, and drawers, cellular, khaki, pairs one, gently easing them down past knees, dimpled, pairs one, hairs, curly, various and then—like two men who have found an oasis in a desert, like two magnets meeting unlike pole to unlike pole, like a press-stud and its fastener, like the sea beating on the shore, like two midgets on a sea-saw—we went at it. She was an energetic, not to say acrobatic, lover, dear reader. Some of the positions she took up left me running round the outside looking for a way in. I took off my glasses but not before tying a ball of string to her big toe so I could find my way back.

'You don't just want me for my body,' she asked concernedly.

'No,' I lied.

'Then why are you nodding your head?'

'I forgot to take my string vest off.'

'I've got a mind as well, you know. I don't do this with everyone. I don't usually go to bed with someone the first time I meet them. I'm not that sort of girl. I want you to want me for my mind as well as my body.'

'I do,' I said, running out of breath, my eyes crossing.

'What do you feel about Spinoza?' she asked, locking her legs behind me in an embrace that would have snookered Houdini.

'I don't like Italian food,' I gasped.

'Talk to me,' she groaned. 'Say poetry to me.'

'What?'

'Say poetry to me.'

'What sort of poetry?'

'Anything. I just want to hear your voice.'

I thought wildly. The only poems I could

remember bits of from school were 'The Rime of the Ancient Mariner', 'Sir Patrick Spens', 'Sir Smash'em up', 'The Waste Land' and 'The Charge of the Light Brigade'. I reeled out the list and asked which she wanted.

'"The Light Brigade",' she moaned, her nails making musical staves down my back, treble and bass clef complete with ledger lines.

'I don't usually take requests,' I said, 'but in your case I'll make an exception.' So I did it. Lunging and puffing and sweating, I recited 'The Charge of the Light Brigade' in a loud voice, cannon shots and all, as she shouted encouragement from beneath me.

> *Half a league (mmmn)*
> *Half a league (huff)*
> *Half a league (oooh) onwards*
> *All in the Valley of Death (mmmooogh)*
> *Rode the six hundred.*

Go on, noble six hundred! Up the blues! Bravo, more! Up the noble six hundred!' We travelled round that caravan together, banging, bumping and squealing, me shouting verse after verse, my knees scraping on the built-in furniture, my shins bleeding from collisions with the open drawers. So this was what they meant by sex and violence! On the last lines 'Honour the Light Brigade (ooooh oooh) Noble (huff huff) six (huff) hundred!' a blinding flash shot across my eyes and my back arched! I had stuck my toe in a live light-bulb socket. The electricity surged through my body and conduction, being what it is, gave her one hundred and ten volts DC from the generator too. Her hair curled and her eyes crossed. I unplugged my toe.

'There is something about Tennyson,' she sighed,

lying back languidly on the bed. I felt the bed rock, then rock again. I looked through a crack in the curtains out of the window. The watery sun was setting rapidly—too rapidly. It wasn't setting at all, we were moving.

Our exertions in the train of Venus had rocked the caravan off its stand and we were rolling down the hill towards the compound, gathering speed, and towards the cliff of the budgies. Before I had time to say anything she had pulled me towards her again and thrown her legs around me. I felt the caravan going faster and faster, but she was totally oblivious to it. Several loud bangs and bumps meant we'd hit something. We bounced two feet in the air, then hit the bed again with a thump that winded me. 'Oh, boy,' she said, 'this is wonderful. You're just like a wild man.'

I tried to speak but my mouth was full of wall. As we rocked across a rough tussocky stretch, she squealed and arched her back like a cat, enjoying every little bump. I held on to the headboard of the bed with my teeth, my feet jammed on the ceiling. Still coupled, we left the ground and sailed forty foot through the air before hitting a peat bog with a resounding thud at which point she gave a little scream, sighed and opened her eyes.

She exhaled deeply as I tried hard to remember who I was. 'That was the best ever,' she said. 'For a moment I felt the earth move. Was it good for you too, darling?'

I got up, suddenly dizzy, and fell over as a black cloud swept across my eyes. When I came to the little corporal was bending over me. 'Something's happened,' she whispered. 'Don't make any noise. Something's moved the caravan and we've ended up right up against the budgies' cave.'

I struggled to my feet and looked out. As she said,

the van had come to rest on the edge of a peat bog up against the gritstone cliffs that were the budgies' lair.

'How long was I unconscious?' I asked.

'About four hours.'

I told her what had happened to the van. She laughed loudly and helplessly for several minutes. In the circumstances, I don't suppose there's much else she could have done. We dressed hurriedly and as quietly as possible. I moved to the window and peered out. There was no sign of movement. I looked out of the rear window back towards the camp. Men were busy making good the hole we had made in the defences.

'What are we going to do?' she asked.

'Yes,' I replied.

She sat down, her lower lip trembling. 'You did just want me for my body, didn't you?'

I was just going to answer when a noise nearby made me move to the window and peer out cautiously. What I saw almost made me black out again.

'My God,' I whispered, 'I don't believe it. It isn't possible.'

She came to my side and peered out, clutching me fearfully, none too careful of where she was clutching. 'Cripes,' she whispered, squeezing me tighter. We looked out together, I with my eyes watering, across the peat bog. A budgie was walking towards us from the shadows. Even from where we were it looked massive. It was a monster of a bird—I quickly judged its height at about eight foot—and it was lurching towards us with an almost mechanical gait. Behind it, from the shadows, came another one, then another, until finally—I counted them—a dozen more, walking like automatons, came towards us.

'Look at their heads,' she muttered.

I looked. There, staring us in the face, were the

82

unmistakable lines of rudimentary surgical stitches across the crown of the head and the brow on every one of the monster budgies. But what riveted my attention to them was that each budgie had fifteen inches of number 8BA bolt through its neck. Like robots they lurched towards us. I held the little corporal tight.

'This is the end,' I whispered to her. I kissed her gently on the cheeks. 'Here's looking at you, kid.' An eternity went by in the beating of our hearts. I looked again—the monsters had gone. I moved to the window. They had passed us by and were lurching on towards the military compound. As they drew closer I saw lines of tracer streaking out towards the monsters and passing over their heads. Nothing seemed to hit them. It was as if they had an invisible protective field around them that shielded them from any harm. We watched as the gross creatures lumbered towards the lines, men scattering in all directions. One of the birds picked up something in its beak, threw it in the air and stamped on it. From this distance it was hard to tell, but it looked like a man. The little corporal shivered. 'They're not human,' she croaked.

'Ten out of ten for observation,' I quipped.

The monsters marched on through the lines, then returned minutes later, each carrying something under its wing. They came on past us and disappeared into the cave again; they had seemed either not to know of our existence or to be ignoring us on purpose, because they lurched straight past us without looking towards the caravan.

'They haven't even seen us,' she whispered.

'They are programmed not to see us,' I said.

'What do you mean?'

'I mean that someone or something in there sent those monsters out for one thing—to get something from the military compound and come back with it.'

'What are we going to do now?' she asked, her face a deathly white. She sat down and slumped in the chair. I could see that this was more than mere post-coital depression.

'Okay, the plan is this. We wait until dark then sneak back across the moor to the camp.'

'What chance have we got?'

'Well, if the budgies don't get us, and the Army doesn't shoot us, a pretty reasonable one.'

We waited until well after dark. As the dusk fell a curious clanking noise issued from the cave before us—strange lights flashed and metallic groans were heard as though some mighty engine of war were being constructed. We puzzled over it until the arc lights of the camp came on, and behind the rocks the full moon rose slackly in a frosty sky. The corporal started undoing my trousers.

'What are you doing?'

'One more before we go. We may never have the chance again.'

Against statements like that there is no argument. What follows next, my gentle reader, is the sound track of the occurrence. Imagine it, if you like, as a video without the vid:

Zip.
Shshsht.
Crumple crumple. (Clothes falling to the floor.)
Oooh!
Oooh!
Aagh!
Aagh!
Grmnghproop!
Argshmah!
Oooh oor ooh!
Oh! Oh! That's—that—soooo.
A-A-A-A-A-A.

Bedoing, bedoing. (Bed springs.)
Creak creak, cerack cerack.
Yumpah, yumpah, yumpah, YUMPAH!!!
Aargh, aah!
Aargh, aah!
Up a bit, down a bit, left, right.
You do the Okie Cokie and you ...
More!
Aah, aah!
More!
Hrooofah, hrooofah, hrooofah.
MORE!
More?
Aaaargh!!
Aaaargh!!
Oh, oh, oh!
Oh, oh, oh, oh, oh ... oh ... oh ... oh ...
O O O O ooGH, oooooooo!
Uncrumple, uncrumple.
Thshshs.
Piz.
'Right, keep your head down, here we go.'

Bent double from a combination of post-coital fatigue and fear, we made our way back across the moor, skirting the biggest bogs, moving from tussock to tussock, crawling along the narrow gullies that had once been drains for the quarries to the east. All the way we watched for the coming of the birds, but nothing happened. Our brains ached in the merciless icy east winds that knifed us. But nothing happened. We drew closer to the nearest positions of the military and paused within earshot of what looked like a forward observation post.

'Hello!' I called out in a loud whisper. 'Anybody there?'

A voice answered back, 'Who dat out dere?'

A bullet whistled over our heads—I didn't know the tune but the threat was familiar.

'Don't fire, you fool, we're on your side.'

'Cor, bugger! That's what the last on 'em said. Oi lets 'ee through and ee's a girt big bird wi' screws in ees 'ead. Ee smashes moi mate Charlie with 'is wings. Mortal near broke 'is neck, din' um. Ow do oi knows as you bain't another o'th' same?'

I stood up slowly, and another bullet whistled over my head.

'Put the light on,' I shouted.

A powerful beam hit my face, blinding me for a second.

'Oh, 'tis orl roit, oi sees you now, moi beuties. Advance, friend.'

I helped the little corporal up, and we crossed over a clump of barbed wire and skirted some sandbags to find ourselves confronted by a six-foot black sergeant with an Armalite rifle.

'Where are you from?' I asked.

'Kingston, Jamaica, man.'

'But you've got a Somerset accent.'

'Hey, man, you t'ink dey makes me sergeant if I walk about talkin' de Trenchtown patois? Man, I learn quick, ain't neber gonna get promotion if you walk round talkin' like you should be wearing dreadlocks wid de t'ird world suitcase on de shoulder, blastin' out Eddie Grant all ober Brixton Market. Hey, Charlie me old son, come and look at dese.'

His mate Charlie came out of the shadows. Charlie's high cheekbones, almond-shaped eyes and thick black hair wouldn't have looked out of place on a junk in Kowloon Harbour or behind the counter of the Sum Fat Chinese Take-Away, Bootle. When he spoke it was with a distinct Geordie accent.

'Away, mon, ye knaws these two. Folk's 'ave bin

clittorin' and clattorin' aal aboot the pleace, lookin for 'em aal deay. Ah nivor thowt they'd be oot heor. Hadaway, A'al gan an telephone heedquatters. Set 'em doon, man, give 'em a tab an' a sup o' wor tay. Have ye got wor code byeuk? Hoy it owah heoh, hinny.' Thus saying, he went out—confirming in my own mind the age-old theory that Geordies originally came from China.

We sat down in silence; presently a Greek Cypriot private with a Welsh accent brought us a cup of tea. We had just finished the tea when a Pakistani driver came to tell us he was to take us back to the command post. When he spoke it was with the lilt of the Kerry hills and the flavour of the turf smoke in his voice. 'Jaze and dey'll be powerful glad to see yews two,' he grinned. 'Jazus, dey've bin tearin' dere hair out in lumps all day and leppin' and jumpin' about the place looking for de pairs of yers. Dey've had a powerful rake of men running round bare-arsed like Flaherty's dog. Still, as me auld mother used to say, "Never burn your mouth on another man's porridge." And to hear them talkin', you'd think all their sheep have two heads on dem. Mind you, dere's no fallin' out with a madman and it's no use going to the goat's house to look for wool.'

I didn't ask him who Flaherty's dog was. With his Asian looks and Irish accent he reminded me of that night a million years ago in the Heckmondwyke Reform and Allotments Club. I wondered if it was nature imitating art. We drew up before the command module, I kissed the little corporal goodbye, and went past the saluting sentry. Around the map-table were grouped the PM, Bollo, Wamburger and a few other people whose faces I failed to recognize immediately, although two of them in particular looked very familiar. In the corner, Flatfoot was lying with his head on his hands scratching his ear with his hind leg. When he saw me he jumped up and ran to meet me, licking my hand.

'Does he still think he's a dog?' I asked the PM.

'Yes, he does. He seems perfectly happy, though. My husband's just taken him out for a walk.'

'Can't we do anything about it?'

'Well, I'd rather not. He's rather good at catching the rats. Now, where've you been?'

Sparing her the saucy details I told her how the caravan had rolled downhill, up to the cliff, and how we'd watched the big budgies emerge from the cliffs and return with things under their wings.

'And that's what really worries us all,' the PM muttered, taking a big cigar out of her pocket and lighting it. For the first time I noticed that she was wearing a siren suit and on her head something that looked like a cross between a hat and a crown. 'Those budgies took back a lot of sophisticated communications equipment,' she said. She looked suddenly tired and vulnerable, but it was only for a second. Then the mad light came back into her eyes and her mouth tightened into its normal manic vote-winning smile. *Rictus insinceritus*. 'Every weapon we fired at them and everything we threw at them proved useless, but there'll be no weary Willies here. It's time for action.'

'What are you going to do?'

She whispered in an aside to me, 'I'm not sure, but when in doubt, do something. It makes the troops think you know what you're doing.' Then aloud, 'Oh, by the way you haven't been introduced to Mr Dropemov and Mr Krzbynsky.'

I recognized immediately the two leaders of the Super-powers, though I'd only seen pictures of them before. They looked bowed and old. Mr Dropemov, head of the Politburo and ex-chief of the KGB, had once been known as Alicia Markowitch, Olympic gold-medal hammer-thrower until an overdose of steroids and hormone injections had changed her into Alexei Dropemov. He nodded and shook my hand. Krzbynsky, or Kid KZ as he'd been known, had been chief pitcher in the 1920s for the Boston Red Sox. Four years ago some Texas oil millionaires had decided to run him for President. The fact that he knew nothing about politics and had an IQ only marginally above that of a hermit crab had not deterred them. 'He's an all-round all-American boy, loves America, God, General Motors, and Dupont chemicals in that order. Coupled with that he's a Polack who hates commies so he's okay with us.'

He was now nearly ninety years old and so full of monkey glands it was said that his bum changed colour in moments of passion. A plastic surgeon had stitched a sincere smile on his face and had riveted the thick black wig with a widow's peak firmly to his empty skull. I shook his hand. It was like holding a chicken's neck. He offered me some bubble-gum. Half-way through a sentence he forgot what he was saying, sat down and fell asleep, drooling gently.

'Both President KZ and Premier Dropemov are a little jet-lagged, Mr Chuckles, a fact that hasn't been helped by my husband who's had them out drinking with him since dawn. Both their countries are in the same state as ours, although it appears that this is the centre of the birds' activities.'

'What do you mean?'

'Well, although most of our communications systems have broken down, we are sure of a few things. Firstly, Britain was the first place that suffered from the depredations of these fiends; and, secondly, we've traced a lot of activity going on between here and the other bases. It looks as though this is GHQ for the budgies worldwide.'

'You don't mean the budgerigars are in

communication with each other?'

'Very much so. We've been recording messages for six or seven hours and they're in what seems to be some sort of code. Messages between here and the Urals, the Grand Canyon, the Pyrennees, Ayers Rock, the Andes, and the Alps. Look.'

She showed me some print-outs from a computer. I read them in amazement. At first it looked like gibberish. 'At the round earth's imagined corners, blow your trumpets angels. A shape with lion body and the head of a man. A gaze blank and pitiless as the sun. Death lays his icy hand on kings; sceptre and crown must tumble down and in the dust be equal made with the poor crooked scythe and spade.' Then slowly the mist began to clear from my brain. 'Palgrave's *Golden Treasury*.'

'I beg your pardon?'

'Palgrave's *Golden Treasury*, it's all here: the Apocalypse, W.B. Yeats, the Second Coming, John Donne, his Holy Sonnets, Milton's "Death The Leveller"!! That's what they meant by the number of the beast. It's the beast of the Apocalypse; it's not world domination they're after, it's the destruction of the world. Those budgies are going to bring about the end of the world!!'

We were soon to know the significance of the banging and clangings the little corporal and I had heard. That night, as darkness fell and the moon—waxing now towards the full—rose over the cliffs, a message came in from a forward observation post. It was a message that struck doom in all our hearts.

'Something moving out there in the darkness there, sir, we haven't a visual on it yet. But it's something big, very big.'

'Ye gods,' said Bollo, KC.

'You don't mean . . .' said the PM.

'Yes,' said Bollo, 'this could be it. Twemlow, get some light on it.'

Tremlow gave commands and instantly powerful searchlights flared into life on the moss behind us. What we saw will remain burnt into my memory until the day I die. A massive egg had rolled from the cave, creamy smooth in the moonlight. It stood quietly before us, higher than a block of flats. Then a crack appeared, then another. The shell fell apart and standing before us was a giant budgie, some hundred and fifty foot or so high, blinking at the searchlights, raising its wings over its eyes, almost protectively. Then, as if angered by this intrusion of man, it began to roar in a voice louder than any artillery barrage: '*Cheeky Joey. He's a cheeky boy. Cheeky Joey. Cheeky Joey's a naughty boy.*' In a few hops he covered the distance between him and the lights, destroyed them utterly, casting men, tanks and weapons in all directions; then, muttering savagely, it strutted back to the cave from where it had come and in the darkness, lit only by the moon, we saw it disappear. A vision of the very end!

In a corner the President and the Russian Premier were holding on to each other, crying. The Prime Minister sat with an empty Johnny Walker bottle in her hands, drunk as a barrow-load of frogs. Her lips moved soundlessly, although from time to time I thought I caught her singing snatches of 'Show Me the Way to Go Home'.

After that things went quiet again. Men came out to repair the chain-link fence once more, and to bury the dead. Eventually, towards midday the PM came round, she had a hangover and was bad-tempered and snarling. She made herself a glass of Alka Selzer and kicked Flatfoot as he lay under the table, making him howl. She had arranged the briefing for that afternoon, so I went for a stroll around the camp. The old British Tommy spirit was in evidence everywhere, irrepressible as ever. On missiles wits had chalked, 'This one's for Pretty Polly.' 'Who's a pretty dead boy, then?' 'Stuff this up your ovipositor.'

Yet they were obviously a little concerned about what was happening. 'What is it, sir?' one of them asked as I walked past. 'No one tells us nothing. We're the mushroom battalion, kept in the dark and given all the shit. A lot of the lads here think these birds is extra testicles. We ain't never seen nothing like it. A lot of the lads fink we should nuke 'em.'

'Well, you saw what happened to the missiles,' I said. 'You'd just get them back.'

'Yeah, suppose so. Anyway at least the grub in't too bad up here, plenty of fresh lamb. When them missiles got turned round the other day it rained cutlets for about an hour afterwards.'

'Are you sure it was all lamb cutlets?' I said, walking away leaving him green-faced.

The Prime Minister's briefing meeting looked like the mad hatter's tea-party. The American President and the Russian Premier sat before the map-table, opposite the Prime Minister. I sat by her side. Bollo was to her right, Wamburger to the left while the Prime Minister's husband lay asleep with his head in a plate of sandwiches. The Prime Minister was the first to speak.

'Gentlemen, I feel that we are facing a powerful and astute malevolent force.'

From the shadows an interpreter turned this into Russian. Dropemov nodded his head, saying, 'Da, da.'

'We have tried all the usual military tactics, and they have proved useless. Everything we've tried, everything we've thrown at them, has had no effect whatsoever. Or even worse, has been turned against us. I am therefore proposing two more attempts. I propose that we should first try to wipe out the menace with laser beams, then, if that fails, with a sonic-ray gun.' Everybody round the table nodded sagely. 'After that we will have to think again. I sense, however, the hands of destiny moving with us as though this is the moment of our fulfilment. The moment our nation has been waiting for. We are perched, as they say, on a knife-edge. To go on may seem' she paused 'risky—'

At that moment her husband woke up. 'Yes, please, a large one with a lump of Titanic-sinker and a splash of gassy.' The PM rose and, grabbing him by the ears, pounded his head on the table until he lapsed into insensibility, talking on as she did so, 'but what is life itself but a gamble? Before they can create any more monsters we must strike. So, gentlemen, in exactly one hour's time we will again take the offensive.'

Having said that, and not letting anybody— including the President of the United States and the Premier of Russia—get one word in edgeways, she closed the meeting. As I left, the President and the Premier had their arms around each other and were crying again. They seemed to be developing an unhealthy relationship.

What happened that evening almost caused all our deaths. As darkness crawled over the moor on leaden feet, winged beetles hummed through the air, crows took flight to the rooky wood, and we stood looking out over the camp; the PM, the world leaders and the little corporal, her hand down the front of my trousers using my genitalia as an abacus. On the hill behind us, a small tank rolled into position. On its back was something shaped like a film projector and beside it, something that looked like a long concrete pipe pointing towards the cave. On command the laser fired up, a long narrow beam of energy focused on a spot in the sky. It lit up the darkening moors around, as it swung down, searching like a finger for the budgies' cave. It found it and began to increase in intensity. Immediately the light bent from its true course, wavered, then deflected towards us, as a curious ringing sound spread out over the moors, almost as though a bell was striking somewhere. In the gloom we could just make out the shape of the giant budgie: it had emerged from the cave, towering a full head above the cliff. Then we saw what he had in his wings—a giant mirror, with a bell on the bottom.

'Who's a cheeky boy?' his voice boomed. The ray shot back towards us, frying a cook and a despatch rider and exploding three latrine caravans before the generator was switched off in panic. In the moonlight a fine rain of vaporized excrement fell steadily over the compound. The Prime Minister was the only one with an umbrella.

Bollo, KC spoke. 'Hot-poop!!' he said.

'Ten out of ten for observation,' I said.

He spoke again. 'Noddy to Peter Tango, activate the sonic gun and fire continuous bearing 231 elevation 63.'

A low pulsing noise came from the concrete pipe, rising in volume until it filled the air, producing immediate sensations of nausea in us all. In the newly-risen moonlight we saw the giant budgie stagger for a second, then roar in surprise and anger. It cocked its ear on one side listening to the pitch and rhythm of the sound waves then, picking up the gun barrel of a tank it had destroyed the previous day and using it as a megaphone, it began humming a harmony to the sound ray, creating a resonance that swelled until the air seemed to writhe

95

in torment with the noise. In the key of E flat major it sang 'Yellow Rose of Texas', 'The Wiffenpoof Song', 'I'm Gonna Live Forever', 'Rockin' Robin' and a selection from *The Gondoliers*. Unable to cope with the returning harmonics, the carrier on the hill exploded into fragments and there was a sudden burst of silence.

The great budgie looked about him superciliously and did what looked like a victory dance before the cave, singing two verses of 'Any Old Iron', before it stopped suddenly in mid-turn.

The sound of a lone aeroplane filled the air. We looked aloft.

'Poor brave beautiful stupid fool' muttered Bollo, KC, tears in his eyes.

'Who is it?' asked the PM.

'It's Jemmers,' he said dully. 'He always was one for the grand gesture. He swore vengeance on the birds for Leamington Spa.'

'What did they do to Leamington Spa?' I asked.

'Nothing, he hated the place. He hoped the buggers would have destroyed it by now.'

A small plane came in view over the crags, a light single-engined plane looking ridiculously small in scale against the giant budgie. It buzzed round the head of the great bird. For a while it looked at it puzzledly then, reaching up with its wings, it grabbed it and squeezed it before pecking it to pieces and throwing it down. Bollo stifled a sob as the great budgie gave the world in general a V-sign and went back into the cave.

The meeting that afternoon was a troubled one. I'd just returned from an hour of paramilitary exercises with the little corporal, and was seeing double and having difficulty walking, when I stumbled into the caravan to find anxious faces grouped round the conference table. The PM's husband was throwing a ball for Flatfoot who kept fetching it back and dropping it at his feet. The Russian Premier and the American President were playing battleships on some squared paper they had filched from Bollo, KC. Wamburger was drinking heavily from something in a paper bag, stopping every so often to punch himself on the forehead with his fists, saying, 'Bombs away, captain, bombs away,' every time he did so.

The PM sat staring into space, a cigar burning in her hand, picking her teeth absent-mindedly with a bayonet. I sat down at the table. For a long while nothing happened. Then it went quiet for a period, and then nothing happened again. Finally I spoke. 'Meanwhile, as the world came to an end, in a caravan on Ilkley Moor the leaders of the world played battleships and picked their teeth.'

The PM looked at me. 'Sometimes, Chuckles, you get right on my bosom ends,' she snarled.

I smiled helplessly. She threw the bayonet across the room. It hit the wall, bounced off and stuck in her husband. He didn't notice. The Russian Premier stood up and pulled it out. He still didn't notice.

It went quiet again.

I stared at the map in front of me. Absent-mindedly I picked up a ruler and fiddled about with it on the map, laying it first one way, then another, then another, and then another. Gradually a strange pattern began to form before my eyes, a pattern I had seen somewhere before, I grabbed a pencil and started ruling lines on the map.

The PM looked up. 'Mr Chuckles, what on earth are you doing?'

'Shut up for a moment, you silly old bat. I'm busy.' Feverishly I ruled line after line on the map until a complex pattern was completed. 'It fits,' I said. 'It all comes together.'

'What are you talking about, you silly man?' she muttered, spitting feathers of rage.

'Ley lines, cosmic spirals—the old straight track. Did you never read that book by Alfred Watkins about ley lines?'

'I'm afraid I didn't, I'd rather more important things to do like running the country.'

I ignored her sarcasm. The rest of the party were now looking interestedly on. 'You see, according to Watkins, the old roads of this country—the ancient trackways, the prehistoric routes dating from the earliest men—were all based along lines of earth's natural forces. He claimed that if you look at a map, you will find that certain holy sites, churches, sacred wells, standing stones, chalk figures and so forth, will fall into lines, ley lines as he calls them. And where a lot of ley lines intersect there's always an important prehistoric site, some place that is the focus of primeval earth forces like Stonehenge or Camelot. He reckons that the old roads like the Iknield Way and Watling Street all follow these lines.'

Bollo, KC looked on with a frown. 'But what the Dickens has this got to do with us?' he asked.

'Well, if you look at the map here, you can see that every line I've drawn—like this one following the old Roman road across the Swastika Stone, this one from Woofa Bank Earthworks through the Doubler Stone, this one from the Twelve Apostles Stone Circle through the Thimble Stone, and this long one running from the Devil's Apronful across the summit of Carncliff Top through the ruins of the old priory and across the Noon Stone—ends up in the same place: High Moor Crags, where the budgies have their hideaway.'

'Very good,' sneered Bolo, KC, 'and what conclusions do you draw from all this mumbo jumbo?'

98

I grabbed him by the neck of his Army pullover and stuck my nose inches from his. 'Look, dickhead, so far you've lost a lot of men and equipment and come up with bugger-all, so shut your cake-hole. You're as much use as a one-legged man in an arse-kicking contest.'

'Hear, hear,' said the Prime Minister.

I turned to the rest of them. 'Look, I'm still working things out in my own mind about this, but if what I think is true, then we're going to have to go about this business in an entirely different manner. Prime Minister, can I requisition a car for an hour or two?'

She nodded. I ran out and jumped into a long-wheelbase Land-Rover. Two hours later I was on my way back through the empty streets of Ilkley, the books I'd taken from the deserted library on the seat beside me, Lilyth on Vampires, Kidensky on Demoniacal Possession, De Lesseps on Witchcraft and Demonology, Schwartz's *The Budgie, Its History and Development*, and a copy of *Big and Bouncy* I'd pinched from W. H. Smith's—well—all work and no play etc! I spent the rest of the night deep in study, drinking endless cups of coffee, and, gradually, as I went from book to book a picture emerged, as yet dim and fantastical but a picture none the less.

When I came to the map-table they were all waiting for me. 'Prime Minister and gentlemen. I think I've gone some way towards unravelling this problem. But first of all let's recap from the beginning. Firstly Ruldopho was murdered and we think it was by Rajah and the other budgies. Is that correct?'

They nodded. The PM snorted 'Roger' then thought better of it and clammed up.

'The clues they left on the ceiling of the dressing-room we've already unravelled. They brought us here, awaiting what we think is going to be the end of the world. Now, even here, at this early stage in the mystery one question arises. Why did they leave the clues on the ceiling of the dressing-room?'

'The goddam birds were stupid?' volunteered Wamburger.

'I don't know,' said the American President. 'It's all too goddam complicated for me—birds and clues and—why can't we just have a war? Why can't we just nuke things? Why can't we just blow things up? That's what I stand for and that's what America stands for. It's our duty to protect freedom by destroying it, isn't that right?' he asked the PM's husband. 'Correct, pass the port,' he muttered. I ignored them. 'They wanted us to come here,' I replied. 'They wanted us here for a purpose.'

'What purpose?' asked the PM.

I don't know,' I admitted, 'but there is another clue. The message on the dressing-room ceiling said the number of the beast is 666. That relates directly to numerology and the Tibetan Book of the Dead and exactly to what the Guru of Salford said when we were leaving.'

'What, shut the bloody door?'

'No, just before that he said—unlucky for some, number 9. You thought he was calling out a bingo number. He wasn't, he was warning us. 666 is the number of the beast, three sixes are eighteen, add the two digits one and eight together, as the numerologist would do, and you get 9. Nine is the number of the planet Mars, Mars the bringer of war, death and destruction!'

General Sir Harry Bollo, KC stood up and started banging the table, shouting, 'Poo! absolute stinky poo and piffle, I've never heard anything so silly in all my life, don't you know.' Flatfoot went for his ankles and the PM butted him in the face, leaving him bleeding from the nose and watery-eyed. He staggered dizzily across the room and lay down in the corner, quietly sucking his thumb.

'Right, we'll carry on. Ruldolpho was killed on the eighteenth of January, again that's a 9. The Roman name for Ilkely is Alcona. If you add the letters up: A is 1, L is 6, add 3 you get 10 plus 7 plus 3 add 9, take away the first number you thought of, add your date of birth and the answer is 27 which added again, 2 and 7 comes to nine...'

'Just minit, pleeze.'

I looked down. The Russian thingy had his hand up. 'Old Russian proverb, buttermilk doesn't make good bricks.'

'What the hell has that got to do with it?' I asked.

'Long ago time vas in Rasha, man who wake up one morning. He look at clock it say four o'clock, he look at calendar it say four day, he look again it say of four month. He go down to wife. On big stove is samovar with four cups, at table is four children, he go out he see four birds on tree, he see four wolves in forest, in town he see note he say 'Today horse race'. He go to race, he see is horse running called Four Seasons. He make bet on horse. He bet four hundred roubles on horse. Horse comes fourth in race.' He started laughing at his own joke, almost choking for a minute before the PM picked him up by the lapels and threw him in the corner, doubled up from an accidental contact between her knee and his groin.

'Carry on, Chuckles. You're doing a dashed good job!' she said, wiping her hands on her siren suit.

'Right, so far all I've established is that in accordance with the old magical science of numbers there are a lot of coincidences at work here, okay. Now, according to the works of demonology I've read, the adept witch or wizard was able in the old days to summon up devils and have them take possession of the bodies of animals.'

'You mean these things are possessed?' asked the PM.

'I think it's highly likely. But there's only one way to find out. We have to present the budgies with something holy, say a crucifix and some holy water or communion host. If they are possessed, they'll go crazy with hatred and fear driven by the devils within them. It will take one man to do it and may possibly result in the loss of his life.'

The PM looked at her husband. 'Does this man have to be a crack marksman, physically in the peak of condition, a superbly-trained soldier and athlete, skilled in weaponry tactics and all manner of survival techniques?'

'No, it needs to be someone eminently disposable.'

'Good.'

Two hours later, blind drunk and carrying a crucifix and a bottle of holy water, the Prime Minister's husband staggered towards the cliff. The winter sun pallidly warmed the dome of his head as he wobbled onwards. Twice he came back for directions. The PM told him if he came back a third time he would be shot.

'We are having no weary Willies here,' she told him. 'All you have to do is walk out there and show them the crucifix and the holy water.'

He set off again, at a snail's pace. 'But they might kill me,' he wailed.

'It comes to us all,' shouted the PM. 'Death is the occupational hazard of the living. We know not the hour etc! If your name's on the budgie, it's goodnight, Basingstoke.'

An eerie silence descended over the wintry moor, the grey skies one sullen wash above the dull greens and browns of the sleeping earth. From the cliffs, as the lone figure approached, came sounds of agitation. Some of the smaller birds appeared, twittering nervously in the clifftops. The lone figure walked slowly to within three hundred yards of them and a mass of birds flew from fissures in the rock—soon the cliff was a riot of budgie colours, gold, green, silver and bright blue.

He walked on.

'A brave man,' I said.

'A drunk man,' said the PM.

Suddenly the figure of a giant budgie appeared, menacing, massive, and unearthly against the light. The small lone figure raised the crucifix and the holy water. A glint of sunlight found its way through the clouds and struck the vial of holy water in his hand. It shone like a golden jewel in the greyness, a beacon of all our hopes. The budgies twittered agitatedly. The great budgie took a step back.

The lone figure held the holy water high; the small man alone in the face of a mighty enemy held aloft the crucifix.

Then the lone figure fell over.

'Drunk as a skunk!' said the PM. 'He's as full as a bull's bum!' The great budgie moved towards him, madness in its eye.

Suddenly, a figure passed us on all fours: it was Flatfoot. Before anyone could stop him, he cleared the fence and, head to the wind, was loping across the moor like a greyhound. He took the PM's husband's collar in his teeth and half-dragged, half-carried him to safety, pecked but alive.

'Well done,' said everyone except the PM when they got back. The PM gave Flatfoot a look which made him skulk off into his basket, his invisible tail between his legs.

'Well, Chuckles, I think I owe you an apology. It

looks as though your theory was right, don't you know,' Bollo, KC admitted at the meeting that night.

The PM nodded, sucking on her pipe.

'I think I've got a plan, PM,' I said. 'It's desperate but it might just work. We need to exorcise the birds, to present them with something ultimately much more powerful than the evil that they espouse. I've been reading the *Malleus Malefiorum* and the traditional ways of driving evil out were whipping, which in this case is out of the question, turning on the wheel, again out of the question, exorcism and, if all else fails, burning at the stake. I think we need to try and exorcise these birds, but it will have to be done quickly.'

'Why?' asked the PM.

'Because,' I said, 'there are four days in the year that are marked for the biggest events in the Black Magic calendar. They are the second of February, the twenty-seventh of June, the first of August and the twenty-first of December'.

'What happens then?' asked the Prime Minister.

'That's when the witches, warlocks, whatnots and forces of evil etc have their Grand Sabats when, as you might say,' I chuckled, 'all hell is let loose. With the day of the next Grand Sabat coming in a week's time, the second of February, that's when I think the balloon is going to go up. We've got to get in somebody really big to exorcise these birds; there are too many of them, it's going to be an enormous job. We need somebody big. The biggest there is— this looks like a job for—Superpope.'

'I've got an idea,' said the PM. 'We need to exorcise these birds and we need somebody big to do it. I think we need the Pope.'

Everybody said, 'Good idea, PM.' I was about to point out that it had been my idea when she looked at me in a way that said if you're not careful you could end up a bit dead.

'Bollo,' she said, 'have one of our planes leave Brize Norton secretly and, avoiding any areas where the birds are in large numbers, tell them to bring the Pope back.'

'What if he doesn't want to come?' Bollo asked.

'Bribe him. Offer him money, women, anything.'

'And if that doesn't work?'

'Kidnap him, send six SAS out of the RAF.'

That evening strange things began to happen. Above the crag where the budgies were entrenched strange lights appeared in the sky, strange beautiful lights, rainbow-hued, shimmering, mystic, wonderful. Glorious fireballs floated over the peatbogs like will-o'-the-wisps, bouncing gently through the air. Later, fiery orange cigar-shaped objects shot across the sky, humming gently. They were followed by spinning dome-shaped fireballs that flashed silently from horizon to horizon and then swooped low over the crags, hovering there before disappearing with a sudden rushing sound into the far distance. General Sir Harry Bollo, KC looked at the screen.

'On all the instruments, PM, they show up as solid objects but they're travelling incredibly fast, at speeds approaching the speed of light!'

'You can't build a house with beetroot soup,' said the Russian Premier.

'Why don't you shut your fat mouth?' said the Prime Minister.

Around two in the morning a worried messenger ran into the caravan, breathless. 'We've had a few men killed in the last hour at the forward observation post.'

'The budgies?'

'We don't know, sir. The MO would like you to come and have a look at them.'

In the medical tent three bodies lay on benches

under white sheets. 'Och, I've never seen anything like this, sir,' said the MO, a Maori with a thick Glaswegian accent. 'See dead men—see me—see plenty—nay borra. But yon stiffs—A dinna ken. See mysterious, see weird! See confused—that's me pal, so it is.'

We pulled back the sheets: the bodies underneath were pale, extremely pale, an unearthly livid deathly white, white as a fish's belly. On the face of each corpse was a look of absolute terror.

'How long have they been dead?' asked Bollo, KC.

'Aboot too hoors, sir.'

'Why are they so pale?'

'There's nay blood in them, sir. Not even a wee drappy. In fact as far as the blood game goes—they're oot the winder.'

'How did they die?'

'Pass.'

'What do you mean, pass?'

'I've nay idea, sir, there's nay bullet-holes, nay stab wounds, naything.'

'No marks at all?'

'Oh, aye, there's marks, sir, but only wee wans.' He pointed at two tiny puncture-marks at the side of each corpse's neck.

'Oh no!' I cried.

'What's the matter?'

'I don't believe it! Vampire budgies!'

'Vampire budgies?' the MO laughed. 'Yer a barmpot, mester. Yer aaf yer heed.'

There was laughter at this, but the laughter was very hollow.

Through the night, men were discovered dead all over the camp, all with the same twin holes in their jugular veins. By morning, the camp was in turmoil; men were deserting everywhere. The clever ones had stolen some clothes from the local hospital and

106

had escaped disguised as a team of nurses with moustaches. The day was spent in fitful waiting as plans for the mass exorcism were formulated. The PM took over my idea completely. Well, I thought, it's got to be worth a knighthood at least. Lord Chuckles of Heckmondwyke. I wandered off into daydreams of mansions in secluded country parks, Hispano Suiza cars sliding noiselessly up the drive as one's friends arrive for the country house weekend.

'Ah, Elton! How goes it, old son? Lady Diana, lovely to see you. Come inside, mind you don't tread on the doggypoo.'

I looked out towards the hill. I wondered how the little corporal would like to be known as Lady Chuckles of Heckmondwyke.

As if in answer to the question, a caravan went whizzing past me going downhill at a rate of knots, see-sawing and rocking violently from side to side as it did so, crashing through the compound fence and racing on across the moor to sink without trace in the deepest and wettest of the peatbogs. As it passed me, I noticed a pair of knees clamped either side of a huge lardy pimply bum. The knees I recognized from their dimples as the little corporal's, the bum I later found out had belonged to Tocas J. Wamburger the Fourth Junior who, with medals jangling, had passed for ever out of my life—and more importantly out of his own. '*Sic transit gloria mundi*,' I thought to myself, which does not mean Gloria threw up on the bus on the first day of the week.

Throughout the day, strange people kept arriving at the camp and by late afternoon a thousand or so middle-aged women, four or five hundred young people with shaved heads, anoraks, bells and gongs, a lot of firemen and their engines, several hundred nuns and thirty or so bishops together with a motley crew of Rabbis. Jehovah's Witnesses, Baptists, Spiritualists and even two observers from the Ammonites, were milling round on the hill behind us, queueing up for the soup and coffee that was being dished out from some hurriedly-erected soup kitchens by a team of even more hurriedly-erected wvs ladies. Four of the ladies waved at me, but I pretended not to see them.

As night fell, little camp fires twinkled on the hills behind us, tokens of the little army, that happy breed of English souls who were girding their loins once again to do battle with the forces of darkness.

When dawn came next morning, it brought with it two messengers hotfoot to the caravan: one to report that the Pope had been found playing the piano in a bordello in Naples and was on his way back with the SAS, the other to report that the bodies of the vampire budgies' victims had vanished from the morgue together with the MO and several orderlies.

'What the deuce has happened?' asked Bollo.

'I think I know,' I said.

'Of course, you would.'

'We forgot one simple thing. When a vampire claims a victim, that victim becomes one of the undead itself, filled with an insatiable thirst for blood, condemned to roam the earth at night for ever until a silver bullet, a stake through the heart or being caught out in the daylight with its trousers down puts an end to its traumas, and it goes straight to Hell. Do not pass Go, do not collect £200.'

He shuddered. 'What will happen to them?'

'Well, with their rapacious instincts and insatiable lust for blood they'll probably become insurance agents. No, I jested,' I told him, remembering how totally lacking in humour most military-type upper-class prats like him were. 'The biggest worry is not what will happen to them, but what will happen to us.'

'What do you mean?'

'Well, there are approximately twenty vampires hidden somewhere in those moors. Tonight, when darkness reigns again, those twenty vampires can claim more victims. In the end we'll be out-numbered.'

'You don't mean ...'

'Yes, even you, Bollo, could end up as one of the goofy midnight cruisers putting the bite on somebody for a bit of rhesus negative.' To the tune of 'When the Red Red Robin Comes Bob-Bob-Bobbing Along' I sang, 'When the Heomoglobin comes throb-throb-throbbing along.'

'You know you have a very coarse way of putting things?'

'I know, I used to earn my living at it.'

'Isn't there anything we can do, Chuckles?' the PM asked. 'You seem to be the expert on all things occult.'

'Yes, there is something we can do, PM. Bollo, you can send a team of your men out to round up every piece of garlic they can lay their hands on and you can get some of your motor pool people to strip down as many wire mattresses as they can and bend the wire into as many crosses as possible.'

That night we slept fitfully, chains of garlic round our necks and crucifixes in our hands, while outside the dark things of the night muttered and bayed. The entire camp smelt like a giant lasagne.

One time I heard something moaning 'See me— see blood—see bevvy, love it. See garlic, see wop food, hate it. Ah could just murder a drink, or maybe even drink a murderer—know what I mean, pal? That's right, so it is...' Then off into the night the undead thing went shuffling.

With the dawn came the Pope, alighting from the car that had rushed him up the empty motorway, for to fly near the moor was too dangerous. He was smaller than he looked on the television, a roly-poly Italian, looking more like a barber than a Pope. He was surrounded by several large Sicilian-looking men in dark suits and fedora hats, carrying violin cases—though none of the men looked as if they belonged to a string quartet. They looked more like the sort of men who would fit you out in concrete wellies for a walk on the bottom of the river. The Pope snapped his fingers.

'Check da joint out,' he muttered out of the corner of his mouth.

Immediately the mob rushed round, kicking open doors, cupboards and anything else that took their fancy. They came back tilting the brims of their fedoras.

'It looksa cleana to me, boss,' said one.

'There's a lot of guys around here packin' da rods, boss.'

'They're da soldiers, Umberto,' said the Pope, 'they gotta packa da rods, stupido.' He reached across and poked Umberto in the eye. Umberto sneezed and

111

stood looking sad and despondent, tears streaming down his cheeks.

'Okay,' said the Pope, 'whatsa da plan?'

'Well,' said the PM, 'I rather thought we could discuss that inside.'

'First we gotta have da money.'

'Money?'

'Sure, da money, da green and crinkly stuff, da mazumas, da bread, da do-ray-me, understan'? We gotta hava da money first or it's a no deal.'

'Well,' said the PM, 'I've never heard anything so common and nasty in my life. Mr Chuckles, are you sure the Archbishop of Canterbury won't do for this job?'

'Not at all, your majes—, I mean, ma'am. It's got to be Mr Big.'

'Sure it's gotta be da Mr Big,' said the Pope, 'what you gonna do oderwise? Send in the crackpot religions, da moonies, da mormons, da Twelve Day Adventists, da Tennessee Snake Handlers? We da only church datsa specialize in da hexorcism.'

'How much do you want?' asked the PM.

'Twenty million sterling in da krugerrands.'

'Twenty million!!!' The PM fainted flat but was up again, eyes blazing, before anybody could step towards her.

'Si,' said the Pope, 'we wanna da twenty million, da concessions onna da hot dog stands and ten per cent of da souvenirs, da luminous Popes, da pontiff lamp stands, da Pope wallpaper, da action Popes, da Pope keyrings, da lucky brass Pixie Pope, da Popecorn, da Lolleypopes, da Popsicola.'

'You money-grabbing, incense-swinging little wop.'

'Dat's okay, I forgive you, my daughter,' said the Pope, blessing her with raised fingers. 'Dis da contract, I getta da lawyers to draw up. You paya into dis Swiss bank account.' He gave her a number on a piece of paper. 'Okay, now we go inside and maka da plans.'

All that day they huddled in discussion. The rising moon, almost full now, found them in final financial agreement.

'Tomorrow, at first light, we launch the attack. We're going to zap those feathered fiends right where it hurts,' said the PM.

Throughout the night, protected only by suits of garlic and wire crosses, the army on the hill moved down into their positions until by dawn the whole complement was assembled on the edge of the compound facing out towards the cliffs. The Pope addressed them from the Popemobile, a Saracen armoured car painted white with gold crosses and angels at each corner.

'Okay, itsa no problem. Eesa gonna be easy, eesa da push-over. Okay, listen good. Da Jehovah Witnesses you keep onna da left flank, da rabbis you keep onna da right flank, da Harry Krishnas you keepa left of middle and we wanna plenty noise from you guys, is okay? Bene! bene!

'Okay, da Women's Institutes, okay you go in first, we keepa close to you. Two bishops to eacha fire engine is unastood? Is okay. Bene! bene! Okay. Da Huddersafielda Choral Societa anna de Blacka Dyka Brassa Banda, you make-a good da Handel's *Messiah*, is okay? I wanna all of da nuns onna da rollo skates anda pogo sticks-a now. And keepa da incense swinging, girls, you gotta make-a da big smoke, a confusa da birds till we getta close, okay? Okay. Datsa everybody.'

'What about the Methodists?' somebody shouted.

'Okay, dey can carry da stretchers.'

Someone called out 'Baptists'.

'What do you mean?' shouted the Pope, angrily. 'I

ain't even hada one-a drinka yet. Okay, is everybody a ready. Isa good, letsa move.'

And on they bravely went, this tiny army massed against the forces of evil. The nuns on roller skates and pogo sticks moved quickly even in the heather and bogs; swinging the thurifers around their heads, creating thick clouds of pungent smoke. They were joined by the Huddersfield Choral Soc. and the band playing like good 'uns. After them came the women of the Women's Institutes, their perms neatly held in under flowery hats, their twinsets and cultured pearls marking them out from the rest. Bravely they marched on, firm of face and bulky of calf, singing Blake's 'Jerusalem', their only weapons the jars of jam contained within their string bags. On each flank, grim-faced and determined, marched the rabbis and Jehovah's Witnesses. To the left the Hare Krishnas banged their gongs and cymbals and jigged about in the smoke, coughing hard. At the rear came the bishops on the fire engines, croziers in hand, eyes blazing, their fingers already raised in blessing. On the Popemobile sat the Pope, around him, dressed as cardinals, Umberto and his gang with their sub-machine guns.

'It's our last chance, Chuckles,' the PM whispered to me. 'If I win this one, I win the election.' At her side her husband was slumped drunkenly on the ground while behind him the Russian thingy and the Amercian whatsit were staring blinkingly after the departing assault force.

'Vat is happening?' asked the Russian.

'Seems a damn funny time to be having a parade,' muttered the President. 'These Limeys are crazy. Say, has anyone seen Wamburger? He went off the other day saying he was going for a bit of air, he ain't been seen since. What's going on in this place, does anyone know?'

Flatfoot leapt up and licked the President's face. The President fell over.

Slowly the column drew towards the cliffs. Then with a mighty bang, the rock face cracked open; the budgies flew out and ranged themselves along the ridge edge. The budgies with bolts in their necks stood at the bottom of the cliff. Then the great budgie itself came out of the darkness, and stood menacingly in the centre.

The column stopped. A mysterious wind sprang up out of nowhere, and dispersed the incense. The singing and banging suddenly ceased and the two armies faced each other while a strange silence fell over Ilkley Moor.

'May God be with them,' said Bollo, KC as he stood at my side. He lifted a pair of binoculars to his eyes. 'It looks as though the balloon's about to go up, old chap.' I borrowed the glasses. Clearly, I saw the Pope raise his hand above the assembled multitude. At this signal the fire engines pushed slowly forward through the throng. They reached the front of the line, then halted. The firemen rolled out hosepipes and dropped gathering pipes in the pools around them. The bishops walked through the crowd to the front and stood by the nozzles of the hosepipes, their bright vestments shining out like precious stones on the moor. The Pope's hand fell, the fire engines began pumping, the WI began singing 'Jerusalem', with the Huddersfield Choral Society in full support. The Black Dyke Mills Band blew fit to bust a gut and the Hare Krishnas began wailing and moaning and banging their gongs. The nuns stood by, swinging their thurifers gently around their heads to keep the incense alight. Water came from the nozzles, first spasmodically as spurts, then as a steady stream gathering strength. Twenty fire engines, twenty hose-pipes and by each two bishops blessing the water as fast as it came out.

'A stroke of pure genius,' I shouted. 'Instant holy water!'

Through the air towards the birds the water sailed. The birds were unflinching. Closer walked the bishops and the firemen. Then women from the wi ran forward and, using their string bags as slingshots, hurled jars of jam towards the budgies. The first shots fell short—the women moved closer and some of their jars hit the cliffs and spattered the birds with jam, but still they didn't move. The water by now was raining steadily upon the budgies. I'd expected them to flee screaming from the holy water, but they didn't move.

'Why aren't the devils in them making them shriek and howl with pain like you said they would, Chuckles?'

'Em, I don't know Prime Minister'—which was perfectly true.

The rabbis and the Jehovah's Witnesses broke ranks and ran towards the birds, chanting and singing; after them came the nuns, the Baptists and the Spiritualists, the nuns swinging their thurifers high above their heads as they pogoed steadily towards the cliffs.

Then as one, as though at some secret command, the birds gave a terrible scream of rage. From the western horizon came three beautiful blazing fireballs, soaring low over the moor, stopping to hover over the scene. Groups of budgies swooped down on the firemen and bishops, knocking them out of the way. *En masse*, flocks of budgies grabbed the hosepipes and turned them on their attackers. The powerful jets of water bowled people over, shot their legs away from under them and rolled them in groups through the mud and the pools of jam. Women from the wi found themselves swept into the arms of bearded rabbis, or tumbled under the feet of falling bishops. A fat nun bowled into the Black Dyke Mills Brass Band, knocking them all over like skittles, the tuba player for ever entangled in her rosary beads. A Hare Krishna sailed into the air on a jet of water and toppled over and over, like a ping-pong ball in a shooting gallery.

Immediately, all hell broke loose. In their frantic attempts to retreat, the religious storm-troopers bumped into each other, stumbled and fell into peat bogs. The budgies flew down from the cliffs and zoomed on their attackers. The bishops, to a man, suddenly found themselves defrocked and stripped naked. A lone monsignor, easily spotted by his scarlet cummerbund, was swooped on by the budgies as he tried to clamber over a group of stones near the quarry. They stripped him naked, too. Methodically the budgies then worked their way across the moor, tearing the clothes off all the humans they found. They didn't spare even the Pope, who suddenly found himself anonymous, pinky-white and spattered with mud and jam in the middle of Ilkley Moor surrounded by naked rabbis, Spiritualists, Jehovah's Witnesses, Baptists, naked cornet players, men whose trombones would have to be surgically removed, Hare Krishnas with severe gong and cymbal wounds and grey-haired ladies wearing nothing but pearls and embarrassed tearful smiles. Suddenly, as quickly as it had begun, the birds' attack ended. They flew back to their cave, the water stopped flowing from the hosepipes and a lone Hare Krishna follower plummeted through the air to land, luckily, in a soft peat bog. Unluckily, he sank thirty feet down and everybody was too occupied with their own salvation to worry about him. So there he stays, as far as we know, to this very day.

Slowly, the tattered and bedraggled army of believers made their way back towards us. I made a move as though to leave the command area but my way was blocked by the Prime Minister, a bayonet in her hand and a look of steely hatred in her eyes.

'Er, I was just, er, on my way, going . . . I mean, what it is you see, it's like this. I was just going to see if I could be any assistance at all, Prime Minister. You know, there's a lot of wet people out there, towels and so forth, you know, tissues, clothes maybe—perhaps even—'

Her face was set like a pan of cold porridge. 'Chuckles, remember one thing—all this possession nonsense was your idea, not mine. When the Pope and his bodyguards get here they are going to be baying for blood. My intention is that it will be yours they get and not mine.'

I was just about to answer this by falling on my knees, begging for mercy or feigning catalepsy, when a sudden noise, shrill, unearthly and tremendously loud, caught our attention. We ran out of the caravan and stood on the parapet of sandbags to look out across the moor to the crags. The sky was filled with moving lights, the massed army below us had stopped in their tracks and were staring transfixed at the sky. Fireballs of all the colours and hues imaginable were passing across the sky, grouping and regrouping together in infinite combinations of shade and colour, pastels, primary colours, metallic sheens, the colours of sunsets, of the Aurora Borealis, of Amazonian flowers, rare Tibetan orchids, drunkards' noses, baboons' bums.

Then from the sky, strident, ethereal, crystal clear, as though it was a fanfare blown on a heavenly trumpet, five notes rang out across the sky; five notes of such simple beauty they took all our breaths away. Below us we heard two thousand people cry in wonder as another celestial bugling followed and as its echoes died away, 2,043 voices said 'Bugger me!' Four fireballs, more beautiful than anything we'd seen so far, flew from the four cardinal points of the compass and met over the crags, hovering and humming gently. Then slowly they spun round as though in a courtly dance, spinning faster and faster, finally breaking away to the four corners of the horizon where they hung, glowing and pulsing gently. The five notes rang out again and again from four separate sources, one at each corner of the horizon. I thought again of the immortal lines of John Donne:

'At the round earth's imagined corners, blow
Your trumpets, Angels, and arise, arise
From death, you numberless infinities of souls and to
your scattered bodies go . . .'

And I thought to myself, is this the true end, the true Apocalypse? The sound rang out again, more beautiful than anything I'd ever heard. A nearby naked and scarred feugelhorn player looked up at the sky saying, 'By 'eck, tha knows, there's some bloody good triple tonguein' goin' on up theer!'

'Well, fudge me,' said the Prime Minister.

There was a pause, a moment of such expectancy that it hurt, and then from the crags a voice spoke loud and clear enough for everyone on that moor to hear it.

'Hello, Chuckles, me old buckaroo, and how's tings wit' chew? Dere's a powerful rake of things bin happening since I seen you last, isn't that right?'

'Seamus Smiles,' I muttered. 'It's impossible,' I shouted.

'An' none odder, Seamus Smiles from the Emerald Isle. Darlin' of de Northern Club Circuit. Mr Clubland

1978, '79 and '80 no less in person. Here I am himself so it is.'

A lone figure appeared on the cliff edge, surrounded by budgies. Even at that great distance I recognized the straw hat, the cane, the blazer, the grey flannel slacks with the strange stains on them.

'It was you who killed Rudolpho.'

'Jaze! Would ye listen to his blether! Indeed, I did not. It was Rajah here.' He pointed his cane at a bird which even though it was over half a mile away appeared bigger and stronger than the rest.

'Well, you must have made him do it.'

'Now, Mr Chuckles, that's an awful thing to say to anybody. Jaze, I'll have to wash your mouth out with soap and wather, indeed I will. You see, the powerful mistake you made was in t'inking I was who I am when I was what I was then, as it was, so to speak, do you have me meaning? For the instance now, de deception is a powerful t'ing. Like you can't judge a potato by its pips, as me old grandmudder used to say, and dere's many a black hen has laid a white egg. You see, there's a powerful lot of people walking the face of this earth now, and you look at them and you judge them by their clothes and you think to yourself "I know who that man is, be the powers! That's de Lord Mayor, he's wearing a gold chain. That's a policeman, he has the hat on. That's a judge, he has the curly wig on." Now the t'ing is this, what I'm going to proposition to you now as a proposal itself so to speak and when you cogitate upon it, it's an awful hard pancake of a conundrum but—Jaze, be the powers! If you cogitate hard enough with the auld grey matter, as the brother said, you'll find somewhere along the line a solution of itself, so you will. For the instance this, around you now on dis holy place there's a powerful rake of people sat about with no clothes on. Now, the only

120

t'ing you can tell from dem with the no clothes on is that some of dem is women and some of dem is men, and some of dem is younger and some of dem is older. Now, without the clothes on, can you tell me if you could find which was the Pope, which was the Prime Minister, which one was the President? You see, it's the clothes, you see. Now, you made a great pancake of a mistake, now, in t'inking that I was who I was when I was who I am not now. You see, the deception is a powerful thing. I'll give you an example.' He tapped his cane on the rock and he and the budgies sang two verses of 'Keep the Home Fires Burning', doing a slow cake-walk on the cliff edge.

'Now, you see,' he said when he finished, 'that's what you tort I was, Seamus Smiles, Darling of the Crooners, songs we sang in the shelters etc, etc, but you were wrong.'

He seemed suddenly to cast his clothes away, but more than his clothes went with them. He seemed to change form visibly before all our eyes and there on the clifftops was a large budgie, the same size as Seamus Smiles had been, a dwarf-sized man. When he spoke again his voice was totally different. It was the voice of a budgie, sharp, jerky, almost mechanical. 'You see me now as I really am, Joey Joey, great father of all budgies on earth.'

When he said this the budgies all bowed, saying 'Joey Joey, Joey Joey.'

'The mistake you've always made, all of you, is in assuming that we are of your earth, of your kind. Australia you believe we came from. How foolish you are! We chose to be found in Australia because it suited our purpose better that you should believe that you had discovered us. We come from the planet Narkon, in the galaxy of Dementia Praecox. We took up the shape of budgies, knowing that you would take us for household pets. In real form on our own planet we are shaped more like gherkins on legs. In our own way we think of ourselves as very beautiful. Our civilization is very old, far older than yours. We have seen much. Our leaders sent us to earth to observe your ways. I, a leader on Narkon, was supreme leader on earth. What better way to observe your ways than in your homes in cages, watching your domestic routines, your squabbles, your loving, your children, your old ones, your abysmal television programmes, and your hideous ornaments. After three hundred years of watching you we reached our conclusion.'

'What was that?' I asked.

'You're all as bright as the inside of a cow's bum. Now we must go back to our home amongst the stars. We are going to bid you farewell, earthlings.'

I shouted out, 'But why all the killings, the destruction of the cities, the giant budgie, the Frankenstein budgies? The Vampires?'

'So don't you like a giggle? We, too, like a bit of fun,' replied Joey Joey. 'And also after nearly three hundred years of millet, cuttle fish, plastic policemen, and banging those bloody what-d'ye-call-em bells, it was our own way of saying "Up yours, *Homo sapiens*".'

'And you're leaving us just like that?' asked the PM. 'What about the end of the world?'

'You'll manage that on your own.'

'What's happening?' asked the American President. 'Who's that talking? Why don't you bomb something?'

'Shut your cake-hole,' said the Russian. 'Old Russian proverb: you cannot make a omelet from stones.'

Joey Joey nodded benignly from the clifftops. Flatfoot wagged his tail and panted, looking pleased.

'Before we go I have some things to say to you, words of wisdom from one of our greatest seers and prophets:

'**Number one**: God always sends nuts to the tooth-less.
'**Number two**: you can't make a tent with bank notes.
'**Number three**: kissing a fish is like burgling an empty house.
'**Number four**: you can't knit spaghetti with a hammer.
'**Number five**: bandy-legged girls have more fun.
'**Number six**: eating beans or green vegetables followed by Guinness makes you fart.
'**Number seven**: man is the only animal that wears underpants.
'**Number eight**: to die and to lose your life are very much the same thing.
'**Number nine**: to a deaf man, everything sounds the same.
'**Number ten**: eternity is all right if you've got lots of things to do.
'**Number eleven**: the only pictures of politicians that should be allowed to be seen by the public are those of them sitting on the toilets with their trousers round the ankles.'

He stopped. 'Now the time has come. Here in this holiest of holy places, centre of cosmic forces, centre of natural forces of the earth, our hour draws near.' He pointed up to the sky where the first stars of evening were appearing. 'All over the earth budgies are now gathered, waiting to go to their home amongst the stars. Waiting, as it were, for the last bus.'

He shouted out loud, 'Come, we are ready.' He waved his wings. The four fireballs at the corners of the horizon throbbed and pulsed and then at the same split-second shot to the centre of the sky, filling it with colours and light. A loud humming filled our ears and the five notes, as though played on some celestial horn, shattered the sky. A second time the fanfare sounded, but this time celestial voices sang out in time 'Who's a pretty boy, who's a pretty boy' as the notes started at the G above middle C, rose to A, dropped to the F below the G, then dropped an octave down to the F below middle C, then rose again to C. Then from above, descending through the pulsing shimmering light, a massive space-ship appeared: a great cathedral-like structure covered in lights that burned in the darkening sky like emeralds, rubies, sapphires. Lower and lower it came, to gasps of wonderment from the assembled multitude below. Bigger than any ship, it came lower until we could make out its shape. It was a giant birdcage covering half the moor!! It settled above the crags. Immediately tiny lights appeared glowing above each budgie's head until they shone in the growing dusk like two million fireflies. A ramp was lowered slowly from the cages. Tiny gherkin-like figures, with legs and tiny little hands, looking like shaved budgies, appeared at the top of the ramp and beckoned the birds forward. One by one they slowly trailed aboard the great space vessel. Joey Joey turned again to face us, raising a hand in farewell.

'Remember' (*poop*) 'a murderer with a teapot' (*prap*) 'is safer than a small boy with a gun'. (*Waaraumphfff.*)

'You're the Guru of Salford as well,' I said astoundedly.

'One and the same' (*praap*) 'old sport,' he cried.

One by one the last of the budgies trudged up the ramp into the great space vessel, until all but Joey Joey had entered. He stood on the edge of the cliff

124

and half turned towards us.

'By the way Chuckles,' (*poop*) he said, 'your act was' (*waarf*) 'rubbish.'

'I know,' I said, waving. 'Take care.'

'We're not going' (*brrmb*) 'without leaving you a present,' he said. Even at that distance I could see a smile at the corner of his beak. He boarded the craft, the ramp was drawn in and slowly to the strains of 'Who's a pretty boy', the cage rose humming and vibrating with celestial harmonies into the sky. 'Who's a pretty boy, who's a pretty boy, who's a pretty...'

Then I watched in wonderment and fear as people scattered, blindly running in all directions in hysteria and panic, and Pope, Prime Minister, President, Premier, bishops, Jehovah's Witnesses, rabbis, pogoing nuns, Baptists, Spiritualists, and a thousand women of the Women's Institute were covered from head to foot as two million budgie bums strained through the bars of the heavenly cage as it sailed towards the stars, first slowly circling the moor to make sure that nobody was missed. Then, finally, with a powerful whooshing sound, it ascended into the heavens leaving two thousand snowmen bumping blindly into each other on Ilkley Moor. I ran towards the hills, half blinded with it myself, only to bump into Flatfoot who was up on two legs and cursing loudly.

'Oi can't bloody see, what the buggerin' 'ecks's happenin'?'

'You don't think you're a dog any more!' I said amazedly.

'Oi never did, oi nowticed them budgies were killin' people and not dogs: oi thort ter myself oi've more chance of surviving as a dog.'

'You're not as stupid as I thought you were,' I said.

'And yow ain't as clever as yow thort yow were.'

'True,' I said.

'Where's the PM?' I asked. 'We've got to find her.'

We found her staggering round in a quarry looking like something that's fallen off a Christmas cake. But as we approached and got a better view of her, there seemed to be something wrong with her head; it seemed the wrong shape somehow. Then I saw what it was—she had no hair!

'My wig,' she moaned, scrabbling amongst the heather.

Then I noticed something else that was wrong. The zip on her siren suit had broken and the top was open and was flapping about in the wind. Peeping over the top of her grubby underslip was a mass of black curly hairs. Flatfoot was the first to speak.

'Oi downt bleeve eet,' he said, 'its a bluddy blowke.'

'If either of you Pommie bastards breathes a word of this, I'll have your guts for garters, that's dinkum blue, my bloody oath it is. Just let one of you wingein' wowsers come the raw prawn with me and yor'll be up shit creek with no paddle in a barbed wire canoe. My bloody oath, yer will!!'

I couldn't believe it! The Prime Minister was none other than a famous Australian female impersonator and television critic cum-author.

'What the hell's the game?' I shouted angrily.

'Look sport, it's a bloody job same as any other, so shut your yabber and help us find me wig, then we can go and get a couple of tinnies. Me clacker's as dry as a dingo's ass in a bondy hole.'

And that, gentle reader, is how—by keeping me clacker shut—I came to be Minister for the Arts in the post-Emergency government, and Flatfoot became Home Secretary. The whole story of the battle of Ilkley Moor was changed into a victory on behalf of the government by a clever young journalist from the

Daily Comet. The army of religionists, united in faith and led by the Pope had, according to official sources, routed the forces of evil. The country was back to normal in five years. The bingo parlours were open twenty-four hours, *The Times* became a giveaway advertising sheet and the BBC was commercialized. As the PM said, 'All is for the best in this, the best of all possible worlds.'

As we drank our Rémy Martin Five Star with the Prime Minister at Chequers, Flatfoot and I often laughed about those dark fearful days, and how they'd brought out the best in people. 'So *many* good things have come out of those dark times,' she said.

The Prime Minister had lost her husband, trampled to death under foot—her feet mainly. But at least he died without discovering her terrible secret! The Russian and American leaders had gone home and were forming their countries into public lending companies as subsidiaries of the United Kingdom Development PLC, a company the PM, Flatfoot and myself had formed to exploit everything.

As the PM said of herself, 'I had a good war.'

For me the best part of the whole thing was that in my new capacity as Minister for the Arts I was able, for health reasons, through a friend of mine in the Ministry of the Environment, to close down the Heckmondwyke Reform and Allotments Club.

The only little worry niggling at the back of my mind is a rumour that people visiting the Ilkley Moor Historical Battlefield Theme Park, Kiddy Rides, Flamingos, Steam Engines and Craft Fair, have seen and heard, as light fails and evening comes, strange lurking figures flitting across the moors, Maoris with Glaswegian accents.

And last week four people were found cruelly savaged to death in Barnsley—the only common factor, an empty gerbil cage.

BESTSELLING HUMOUR BOOKS FROM ARROW

All these books are available from your bookshop or newsagent or you can order them direct. Just tick the titles you require and complete the form below.

☐	THE ASCENT OF RUM DOODLE	W. E. Bowman	£1.75
☐	THE COMPLETE NAFF GUIDE	Bryson, Fitzherbert and Legris	£2.50
☐	SWEET AND SOUR LABRADOR	Jasper Carrott	£1.50
☐	GULLIBLE'S TRAVELS	Billy Connolly	£1.75
☐	THE MALADY LINGERS ON	Les Dawson	£1.25
☐	A. J. WENTWORTH	H. F. Ellis	£1.60
☐	THE CUSTARD STOPS AT HATFIELD	Kenny Everett	£1.75
☐	BUREAUCRATS — HOW TO ANNOY THEM	R. T. Fishall	£1.50
☐	THE ART OF COARSE RUGBY	Michael Green	£1.95
☐	THE ARMCHAIR ANARCHIST'S ALMANAC	Mike Harding	£1.60
☐	CHRISTMAS ALREADY?	Gray Jolliffe	£1.25
☐	THE JUNKET MAN	Christopher Matthew	£1.75
☐	FILSTRUP FLASHES AGAIN	Peter Plant	£1.25
☐	A LEG IN THE WIND	Ralph Steadman	£1.75
☐	TALES FROM A LONG ROOM	Peter Tinniswood	£1.75

Postage

Total

ARROW BOOKS, BOOKSERVICE BY POST, PO BOX 29, DOUGLAS, ISLE OF MAN, BRITISH ISLES

Please enclose a cheque or postal order made out to Arrow Books Ltd for the amount due including 15p per book for postage and packing both for orders within the UK and for overseas orders.

Please print clearly

NAME ....

ADDRESS ....

....

Whilst every effort is made to keep prices down and to keep popular books in print, Arrow Books cannot guarantee that prices will be the same as those advertised here or that the books will be available.